I0595415

Theodore Child

Summer Holidays

Travelling notes in Europe

Theodore Child

Summer Holidays
Travelling notes in Europe

ISBN/EAN: 9783337310042

Printed in Europe, USA, Canada, Australia, Japan

Cover: Foto ©Andreas Hilbeck / pixelio.de

More available books at **www.hansebooks.com**

SUMMER HOLIDAYS

TRAVELLING NOTES IN EUROPE

BY

THEODORE CHILD

NEW YORK

HARPER & BROTHERS, FRANKLIN SQUARE

1889

CONTENTS.

With a few exceptions the sketches and notes composing this volume appeared originally in various American and English periodical publications, *The Atlantic Monthly*, *The Cornhill Magazine*, *The Gentleman's Magazine*, *Lippincott's Magazine*, etc. These various essays have no continuity nor any connection of subject; they are simply souvenirs of summer holidays which the author has ventured to reprint in the hope that they may find favor in the eyes of the travelling public, and also of the public that is content to travel in an arm-chair by the fireside.

SUMMER HOLIDAYS.

DOWN THE DANUBE TO CONSTAN-TINOPLE.

I.

AT Buda-Pesth, having for the moment had enough of swift travelling, I abandoned the dusty Orient Express, and, after resting a few days in the delightful Hungarian capital, I proceeded on my way to Constantinople on board one of the Danube steamers, the *Ferdinand Max.* It was in the month of August of 1886, the weather was brilliant, the moon was full, and so we started one Saturday at midnight, and steamed along all night, stopping from time to time at villages on either bank of the river to take in fresh passengers. The next morning I was on deck betimes to inspect the landscape, and the boat, and the passengers. We were in the midst of a very broad stream of dirty yellow water, flowing with a swift rippling movement between banks of brown, clayey

I

earth, eaten away by the wash and crumbling visibly into the river. On either side, here and there, were piles of wood cut and stacked symmetrically, and thickets of willows, and, beyond, forests of pale green poplars stretching away and away over the endless plains and beneath the cold, pale blue sky, sprinkled with white, flakey clouds. After continuing for some time between these sad, green, and silent expanses of willow forests, we came at length to a low sandy island, and then to a group of floating water mills, anchored diagonally across the stream, so that each wheel might receive the full and unimpaired impulse of the current. The floating mill is composed of two flat boats, or pontoons, on the larger of which is the mill and the house where the miller and his wife and children live, while the smaller one serves simply to support one end of the shaft on which the water-wheel is suspended. All down the Danube the presence of a group of these mills is a sign that you are near a village. First of all you see ten to twenty floating mills dotting the stream, then you see a break in the willows, a muddy shore covered with litter and pigs, two or three broken-down victorias drawn by lean horses, a landing-stage, a dirty and picturesque crowd, and then you may know that you have arrived at a station. The first station we touch at this morning is Baja. An old Turk comes on board with various bundles of nondescript baggage.

The landscape continues unchanged until we near the next station, Szekcsö, a village which climbs up the side of a yellow hill running steeply down to the water's edge. This village is a harmony in yellow and white: the hillside is yellow, the cottages are yellow and white, each with a loggia in front and a thatched roof. There are two churches with quaint rococo bulging spires, one painted bright red and the other flaring blue. The bank of the river in front of the village—the marina as we may call it—is a typical confusion of mud, straw, and miscellaneous litter, on which you see flocks of geese and ducks, herds of black swine, ox-carts, oxen, washerwomen, and idle peasant boys, dressed in white short skirts and sleeveless jackets, like true Magyars that they are.

Leaving Szekcsö we find ourselves once more between banks of mud eaten away by the wash, and between monotonous forests of willows. In the brilliant sunshine the smoke from our boilers casts a deep brown shadow on the dirty yellow water, and so we glide along—through plain, sand slopes, and willow forests, and low hills dotted here and there with villages and vineyards, the churches standing out in vivid white *silhouette*, and the river winding and ever winding beneath the immense expanse of sky. The flatness of the surrounding country, the vastness of the river—whose banks rise scarcely a foot above the level of the yellow water—the paleness of the green wildernesses of willow-trees which stretch away on either side as far as the eye can reach, the rareness of villages, the absence of signs of life or of industry, the absence even of birds, all tend to make this part of the Danube very monotonous. The aspect of nature is novel, certainly, but when these same dominating tones of pale green and dirty yellow continue to prevail day after day one grows a little tired of them. The ardor of sight-seeing diminishes, and one begins to look around one for distraction.

The *Ferdinand Max* is a good river boat, with six private deck cabins over the paddle-boxes. The saloons and general accommodation are fairly convenient, the cooking is passable, the officers polite and amiable. The passengers on the first-class deck are all Hungarians or Austrians. The ubiquitous Englishman is represented by the writer of these lines alone. On the second and third class decks the passengers become more mixed at each landing-place—there are Turks in turbans, Magyars in white petticoats, and shepherds clad in sheepskins who wear artificial flowers in their hats.

After dinner I had a long talk with a Magyar, who, being a professor at the University of Buda, was able to tell me much that was interesting about Hungarian history and heroism. With the aid of innumerable cigarettes he rearranged the map of Europe to our mutual satisfaction. His plan was based on an alliance of England, Germany, and Austria against Russia. The allies were to take Russian Poland, divide its territory between the two German powers, drive Russia once for all out of Europe, and leave her to develop purely as an Asiatic power. This excellent patriot ended by pressing me to induce some of my countrymen to establish themselves in Hungary. "We have no industries," he said; "our people are all agriculturists, and, consequently, we have to import all our manufactured goods; we do not even make needles and thread in Hungary. There are great openings in all minor industries, but what we need especially are roads and bridges. Remember that there is only one single bridge over the Danube all the way between Pesth and Petrawardein. Our government even offers a premium to native production; anybody, of whatever nationality, who establishes a manufactory in Hungary enjoys exemption from all taxation for a space of twenty years. There is a great future for our country; in fertility it is a perfect garden, but, as you see, it is not half populated; these forests along the Danube swarm with wild boars and wolves."

By this time other Hungarians and some Servians of the upper classes, who had been educated at Paris and spoke French, joined our gossiping party, and as the Hungarians are vivacious and cultivated people, very advanced in the amenities of life, we had a pleasant time and discoursed of many things.

After passing Vucovar the scenery became less monotonous, and soon we entered a smiling, hilly country, fertile and beautiful as a vast park. Here and there, along the banks, we see open huts of simple thatch, supported on rough timber poles. During the summer the peasants and their families live in these huts, under arms, and watch to protect their crops from the thieves. The regular villages, it appears, are just over the hills on the opposite slope. "Are those Servians?" I asked my professor friend, pointing to some brown-skinned, long-booted, second-class passengers, who were smoking long pipes and playing cards. "Servians? No; the Servians wear shoes. Long boots are for Magyars." I laid the information to heart. How could I have asked such a question? Of course, the long boot is the appanage, the glory, the distinctive sign of the Magyar!

Towards sunset on Sunday afternoon we came in sight of the famous fortress of Petrawardein, a huge, brown, fortified rock, with barracks on the top, and opposite is the town of Neusatz, the first important town since Pesth. Here the Danube is crossed by a railway bridge and a bridge of boats. There is much animation and shouting, and we take on board many passengers in exchange for those whom we land. The view is certainly fine, and Petrawardein doubtless evokes

many souvenirs in the minds of those who are
well-read in history. For my part, being ignorant,
I felt vaguely impressed by the prestige of the
name and by the sight of the casemates and can-
non which, from the heights of this towering rock,
command the river and the surrounding country
in all directions. But, after all, I was still more
impressed with the aspect of the sky when the
sun had sunk below the horizon, and left it all
rent and torn into sheets, and crags, and wedges
of red, golden, and pale green light. And the
broad Danube resembled an immense lake, whose
surface, quivering with minute, regular ripples,
seemed as it were to have a fine grain, and suggested the comparison of an immense skin of sil-
ver-colored morocco leather.

The next morning we arrived early at Belgrade,
having cast anchor during the night at an intermediate station, the moon not deigning to shine
sufficiently to permit nocturnal navigation. The
name of Belgrade is written in strange semi-Greek,
semi-Russian characters. We are now beyond
the confines of Hungary, at least on one side of
the river, which is Servia. At Belgrade we hear
that Prince Alexander of Bulgaria has been driven
out of his dominions ; and, thereupon, we all proceed to rearrange the map of Europe once more,
and to indulge in the wildest conjectures, which
scarcely allow us to remark the scenery of hills
and vineyards, varied with willow forests, which

accompanies us through Kubin and Pancsova as far as Drenkova. Since Belgrade I notice the first-class passengers have become more mixed and noisy. There is a group of Servians who are drinking and talking politics with fury, shouting and stamping like maniacs. Another Servian, reclining full length in the saloon, where the table is laid from morning until night, and where somebody is always eating or drinking, calls ferociously for a cigar. The waiter brings a "Virginianer," and, pulling the straw out half-way, he presents it thus to the young pasha, who takes it lazily, and lights it without a word of thanks to the slave. An hour after noon on Monday we arrived at Drenkova, where we left the *Ferdinand Max* and went on board a small steamer, the river being too shallow and the navigation too difficult for the large boats. Here the fine scenery of the Danube really begins, and if I were to make this journey again simply for the Danubian scenery, instead of taking the boat at Buda-Pesth I should continue through Hungary by train to Bazias, and proceed thence by boat only as far as Turn-Severin, or Lom Palanca, where one finds railway communication. It must be remembered, however, that travelling in Eastern Europe is by no means luxurious or rapid, and that, after all, the slow Danube boat, and the often monotonous Danubian landscape, are far preferable to the fare one meets with when misfortune or defective couplings strand one in a verminous Bulgarian village.

After leaving Drenkova the Danube enters the mountains, and winds along, forming, as it were, a series of vast hill-bound lakes. On either side the thickly wooded hills slope down to the water's edge, and we steam on and on, but there is no exit visible. On the contrary, the hills are closing in upon us and becoming precipitous. We shall certainly strike against the frowning rocks. No; the steamer makes a rapid turn, passes through a narrow gorge, and we enter another vast lake surrounded by hills, which in their turn fade away into a deep blue indigo mist as we advance through the rocky, wooded solitude, enlivened only rarely by two or three fishermen plying their nets from primitive boats. After traversing a series of these seeming mountain lakes, we pass the Trajan's Tafel—an inscription on the rock about which the guide-books are eloquent, and which marks the site of a vanished Roman bridge—and here we are at the famous "Iron Gates," most overrated of curiosities. In this part of the Danube there are rapids and a quantity of small and sunken rocks scattered across the stream, which cause the water to eddy and bubble, and thus enable the impressionable to figure to themselves the "Iron Gates" as a terrible rock-bound boiling gorge. The "Iron Gates" are a delusion and a snare. I am glad the sight of them did not figure even as an item on my Danube programme. Indeed, they left me quite as indifferent as they did that turbaned old Turk who came on board at Baja, and who, while we were passing the "Iron Gates" and straining our eyes to gaze at nothing, was gravely performing his ablutions at the ship's pump according to the Moslem ritual—washing his hands, arms, face, the top of his head, the parts behind his ears, and his big toes, but the latter only figuratively by smearing his wet fingers over his inner shoes. After this lustral ceremony he wiped himself on a large cotton handkerchief adorned with light green and white chrysanthemums on a *café-au-lait* ground, and, having adjusted his turban, he spread out his carpet and prayed—for he was a pious Turk, and five times a day he observed carefully the hours reserved for prayer, and sought "the favor of God and his satisfaction," as the Prophet bade him.

At Kalobo the fine scenery, the mountains, and the lakes came to an end, and the Danube continued to flow broadly between low hills and vast plains. Before sunset we reached Turn-Severin, where we remained all night, having once more changed boats, and having abandoned the little steamer for a roomy river boat called the *Orient*, bound for all the Danubian ports as far as Galatz on the Black Sea. At 5 A. M. on Tuesday morning the *Orient* cast loose her moorings, and we steamed along through soft, velvety landscape between low, crumbling banks of brownish earth. The water was still dirty yellow in color and heavily charged with earthly matter. The " blue Danube " is evidently a myth. I observe that the inscriptions and notices on our boat are written in four languages — Servian, Roumanian, Turkish, and French. The names of the landing-places become more and more illegible, and the appearance of men and things more and more novel, dirty, neglected, and, in a word, Oriental. At Brza Palanka we admired the beautiful undulating country and the rich vineyards on the slopes. On the shore, amidst the usual swarm of geese, pigs, children, and oxen, the peasants stood lazily watching us. Their costume consisted of short white trousers, white blouse, broad waistbands, a jacket of untanned sheepskin with the wool inside, and a conical astrakan cap. Their feet were generally bare, though some wore gaiters and shoes made in fragments and tied on with string and leather thongs. Some of these peasants wore red fezzes. Along the shore and up into the country stretched a long procession of four-wheeled ox-carts with basket sides, laden with Indian corn, which was being transferred into Black Sea boats.

As I go down to breakfast in the saloon I notice among the new passengers a fat woman wearing a red dress of Occidental cut, enormous earrings, and a sort of gold-bound turban. Accompanied by her husband, her sister, and half a dozen grown-

up children, this huge old woman is smoking cigarettes and playing cards. She calls out for the
"kafedjieh," a gentleman who, in return for his
services as interpreter and check-taker for the
third-class passengers, enjoys the privilege of selling Turkish coffee and "raké" on board. The
"kafedjieh" is a recognized and necessary institution on board all passenger ships plying in Turkish waters and in the immediately adjacent parts.
Generally he is a very bad character, but the sight
of him and of his little Turkish coffee-pans and
tiny cups is welcome to the Occidental in quest
of new sensations. So I, too, cried out "Kafedjieh!" and requested a cup of coffee *à la Turque*.
And soon the servile little scamp arrived, like
Agag, treading delicately, carrying the shining
brass pan with the handle protruding at right
angles, and, balanced on the pan, a square brass
tray, and, in the middle of the tray, a tiny porcelain
cup and saucer decorated with insipid blue and
pink ornaments. In the twinkling of an eye this
dainty combination is undone, the brass tray and
the cup is on the table before you, and the coffee
poured into the cup has lost none of its aroma
during the passage from the kitchen to the cabin.
I promise myself to indulge frequently in this
savory coffee during the rest of the journey.

After breakfast I learn from the captain that
the news of the expulsion of Prince Alexander is
exact. It appears that there is a revolution in

Bulgaria. The captain hopes that we shall be allowed to continue our journey, but fears that in any case we shall find communications interrupted at Rustchuk. I light a cigarette and console and amuse myself by watching the huge old woman, who is squatting on deck and holding in her lap a watermelon, which she is excavating with a bowie-knife and distributing in segments to the various members of her family. There is a great consumption of watermelons on board; the shaggy, ragged, brown-skinned third-class passengers seem to live on the cool rose-colored flesh of the *pastèque.*

At Kalafat we are informed that the river is still open, and that we need not fear to go on to Widdin, which is the first station in Bulgarian territory. The scenery is still without interest. Widdin comes within view with its white, low houses, its minarets and its ruined forts, which were dismantled at the conclusion of the last provisional settlement of the Eastern question. The town looks rather ruined and miserable, but the wharf is the scene of great animation and excitement, all about nothing. Several Turkish families come on board with all their household goods and chattels—men, women, and children, all laden with watermelons and grapes and coarse pottery, and flying at the first rumor of political troubles. Some soldiers in white uniforms with exaggerated epaulets, and a miscellaneous crowd of Armenians,

Greeks, and Bulgarians join our boat. And so through the blazing sun we steamed on to Rakhova, a town prettily situated on a hillside terraced with gardens and cottages. But as a rule the scenery continued to be without interest, and the company on board had become very mixed and very noisy. In the evening a lot of Bulgarians began talking politics, and from nine o'clock until two in the morning they howled and bellowed, and finally drew knives. Two champions had a brief engagement at close quarters, and cut each other's clothes, and one received a gash in the forearm before they could be separated. Finally, the revolutionaries calmed down and retired to rest; and when I ventured at last to go to my berth, I found it occupied by one of these hirsute brigands, who was lying on his back, stark naked, and snoring like a threshing-machine. Naturally I did not venture to disturb him or even to appeal to the steward. The circumstances were too delicate.

The next morning (Wednesday) we arrived at Rustchuk at 7 A. M., and found everybody in a state of great alarm. Had we any news? Where was the Prince? What had happened? Telegraphic communication, it appeared, was interrupted; the wires were in the hands of the revolutionaries. Would the train run to Varna that day? "Yes," replied the station-master, "but it is probably the last we shall make up, and when you get to Varna I cannot guarantee that you will be allowed to proceed. I believe the frontiers are closed." This was a pleasing prospect, the more so as we knew we were destined to undergo five days' quarantine before being allowed to enter Constantinople. However, we were soon joined by a few passengers from the Orient Express, and at 9 A. M. we started in the train for Varna, where we arrived after a six hours' uninteresting journey under a broiling sun. No one was allowed to enter the town of Varna. The orders were to get us on board the Austrian Lloyd steamer at once; and so we adventured ourselves in small boats on the choppy Black Sea, scrambled as best we could up the swaying companion-ladder of the *Ceres*, and at five o'clock the next morning (Thursday) we woke up at Kavak in the Bosphorus.

II.

Five days' quarantine at Kavak! Such was the good pleasure of the Sultan ; and however anxious we might be to admire his famous capital, there was no means of escaping the application of this decree. And so, with her quarantine flag at the mast-head, and with quarantine officers in red fezzes to guard her gangways, the Austrian Lloyd steamer *Ceres* took up her anchorage snugly just off the village of Kavak, at the entrance of the Bosphorus, but far enough in to be sheltered from the winds and the waves of the Black Sea. The situation was charming and interesting. From deck we had a view of the prettiest part of the Bosphorus, towards Buyukdere and Therapia, where we could distinguish the summer villas of the ambassadors of the different great powers; astern was the fort of Kavak, built on a sheltering bluff; to the right and the left on each side of the Bosphorus, the villages of Anatoli-Kavak and Roumeli-Kavak, with the remains of old Genoese fortifications and round towers, climbing up the hillside. We might have imagined ourselves anchored in a beautiful mountain lake, for the hills rose all around us, and in the distance seemed to close the winding Bosphorus at each end.

Five days' imprisonment on board this ship! It seemed a long time. Could we not go ashore? Yes, there was a lazaretto; but experienced travellers warned us that the accommodation was of Turkish simplicity. It was better to remain on board and pay the fixed tariff of 15 francs a day. So we all remained on the ship except a fat Turk and his secretary, who were supposed to go to the lazaretto; but, knowing him to be a pacha, we all felt perfectly convinced that, when once ashore and out of sight of the *Ceres*, he simply took a carriage and rode across country, and so, indirectly, to Constantinople. In Turkey you can fare very well if you are a Turk. This pacha was one of the fattest and roundest men I have ever seen. Among his baggage he had a low table, hollowed out in a semicircle, and into this crescent-shaped aperture he slid his majestic abdomen when he took his meals. He could not sit at an ordinary table ; and, on the other hand, when he sat cross-legged in the orthodox Turkish fashion, his dignity spread around him in such voluminous concentric ripples that, had it not been for the ingenious contrivance of the adjustable table, it would have been impossible to place anything within arm's reach of his obese excellency, who would consequently have died of starvation. We regretted the departure of this rotund personage, as much because we felt sure that he was unfairly escaping quarantine as because his presence among us might have been a source of amusement, and amusement was precisely what we most needed, for how were we to pass these five days? In vain one would play the philosopher and congratulate himself on having cultivated, by long years of practice, a natural faculty for doing nothing. In vain another would bring out fishing-lines from the bottom of his trunk, and another books, and another playing-cards, while the ladies appeared with crochet and needlework. Alas! among the first-class passengers there were only four ladies, and we were eighteen men to pay court to them and hold their skeins of wool. There was an English woman, and a Greek woman, and a German woman, besides a venerable old Armenian matron, with whom it was difficult to exchange ideas because she only spoke Armenian.

2

Among the men were Armenians, Greeks, Turkish *rayas* of mixed origin, three Englishmen, a German, a Spanish Jew, and an Italian commercial traveller, who spoke in gentle whines and wished the company collectively "Bon appétit" each time he sat down to table. Well, before the end of the first day's captivity we had broken up into sets, and the women had already "had words" concerning the right of reserving the deck chairs by laying a shawl over the back. As for the sets, the Armenians and the Greeks formed a card-playing and fishing company; the commercial traveller paid court to the proud German, and daily showed his samples to the German's wife; the Englishmen and the Spanish Jew formed a smoking and gossiping set, and amused themselves by observing and criticising the others and collecting and retailing the major and minor news of the ship.

Our chief distractions were the very material joys of four meals a day, followed by hours of beatitude and cigarette-smoking on deck during the intermediate periods of digestion. Then we would watch the new ships that came into quarantine alongside of us, or gaze enviously at the pleasure parties gliding up and down the Bosphorus in swift caïques. For me this five days' station off Kavak was a sort of introduction to Turkish life, and I sat for hours together watching that lovely little village and admiring the picturesqueness of those old Genoese walls and towers. The houses of Kavak are not merely bathed by the waters of the Bosphorus : some of them are built literally over the water, and have their water-gates like the houses of Venice, while caïques take the place of gondolas. Built simply of wood, and painted red or blue or green, these houses climb up the hill amid rich vegetation and gardens, rising terrace above terrace ; and, dominating the tallest trees, are two white minarets with their surrounding galleries near the top. Five times a day we saw the "muezzin" appear in the gallery at the top of each minaret, and heard him call the faithful to prayer in a far-reaching nasal voice, chanting, as it were, a prolonged and melancholy wail. At this signal the pious Turks, who swarmed on our third-class deck, would take their pitchers, and, after performing the proper ablutions at the ship's pump, each one spread out his carpet, turned his face towards Mecca, and religiously said his prayers, yawning, stroking his beard, and prostrating himself to the ground according to the ritual of the Prophet. The venerable old Turk, with whom I had travelled nearly all the way from Buda-Pesth, particularly edified me by his piety. He wore the turban of the faithful who have made the pilgrimage to Mecca, and he was most exact in his religious observances, even bearing on his brow the trace of his piety; for you must know that the Moslem interupts his prayer from time to time in order to prostrate himself and strike his forehead against the ground. It is on account of these prostrations that the Moslem is obliged to wear a head-covering without brim or peak, for it is contrary to custom and contrary to all the rules of politeness to appear bareheaded in public or in any incidents of serious life. But, as the mosque floors are always covered with matting, and as the faithful may be forced by circumstances to pray in all sorts of inconvenient places, the good Moslem will always carry in his pocket a potsherd, which he can place on the floor in front of his prayer-carpet wherever he may be, and so have the wherewithal to mark his brow. My pious Turk carried his potsherd with him. He had also his Koran in a case. And each time after his prayer he brewed himself a cup of coffee over a spirit-lamp, rolled a cigarette, and smoked it with dignity, looking all the time the very picture of calm and venerable felicity.

This third-class deck interested me continually, and two or three times a day I would stroll aft discreetly and glance at this strange collection of Mussulman humanity—men, women, and children reclining or sitting cross-legged or on their heels, amidst a confused mass of carpets, mattresses, bright-colored wrappers, watermelons, earthenware pitchers, and household utensils of all kinds. The women all smoke cigarettes, and all have their faces and shoulders wrapped up in thin white veils. One of them has a cage of doves—a scarlet cage of complicated form, and painted with bright blue and green ornaments.

On Friday, which is the Mussulman Sunday, the Bosphorus was gay with caïques, those wonderful *kirlangich* or "swallow-boats," which are as characteristic of Constantinople as gondolas are of Venice. The caïque is generally made of thin planks of beech-wood, with a neat finish and more or less elaborate carving. It is sharply pointed at both ends; the oars, very thin, wide, and light at the feather end, become thick and bulbous at the handle; the passengers sit in the bottom on carpets or cushions at one end, and at the other sit the rowers, who vary in number from one to six, in which case they sit three on each side. Nothing is more graceful and elegant in aspect and movement than one of these caïques, bearing a burden of fair Turkish ladies clad in silks of every hue, with a fat eunuch at the helm, and six stalwart Nubians in rose-colored jackets pulling at the oars with rhythmic swing. The good people of Kavak also came out in their caïques, or strolled up the hillside and sat under the shade trees, the mothers, accompanied by their children and their handmaidens, gravely draped in "yachmachs" and "feridjis;" some, too, rode upon asses, and the scene was patriarchal and biblic, and reminded one of the promised joys of Mahomet's paradise, which are simply the joys of

life in this little village of Kavak idealized and relieved of the disagreeable accident of temporality.
The Koran, it is true, says nothing about water
promenades in caïques, owing, doubtless, to the
fact that Mahomet never had the pleasure of seeing the Bosphorus and its swallow-boats; but the
Prophet does say distinctly that those who enter
paradise shall dwell in delicious gardens shaded
by fine trees and watered by ever-fresh streams.
The elect, he continues, shall rest on couches
adorned with gold and precious stones; young
slaves of unfading beauty shall pour into their
cups delicious wine, which will not get into their
heads or trouble their reason; ripe fruits and
birds ready roasted will always be within reach
of their hand; they shall hear neither accusations
nor vain discourse; the word peace shall re-echo
on all sides; and, besides the wives he had upon
earth, each of the elect shall be served by at least
sixty-two beautiful young maidens with black eyes
like pearls hidden in oyster shells; and the continual presence of these houris shall be the recom-
pense of the good he shall have done on earth.
To us prisoners on board the *Ceres* the simple
villagers of Kavak, sitting calmly under their
shade trees, or skimming in their caïques over
the Bosphorus, seemed to be already enjoying the
bliss of paradise.   Happily our captivity was
drawing towards an end.   On Monday we counted gayly the successive prayer-calls of the " muez-

zin," and at night, instead of listening impatient-
ly to the wailing cry of the sentries passed from
station to station along the coast, we improvised an
orchestra on deck and had a dance, accompanied
with rockets and Bengal fire, which the captain
brought from the signal stores. Our orchestra
consisted of an accordion, a kettle drum, and a
triangle. The steward performed on the former
instrument; the first lieutenant made an empty
biscuit-tin do duty as a drum ; and the ingenious
captain, armed with a toast-rack and a roasting-
spit, produced silvery sounds similar to those of
the triangle. And so we ended our quarantine
gayly, and on the morning of the last day of August, 1886, we steamed down the Bosphorus with
clean papers, and at last the panorama of Constantinople spread itself in white and luminous
splendor before our eyes.

CONSTANTINOPLE.

I.

THE fuliginous and anti-picturesque mechanism of the steam-engine has certainly an impressive grandeur of its own, but the progress of electricity and of ballooning permits us to hope that it will prove to be only a transitory invention. This hope seems particularly consoling when we find that we have to enter the Golden Horn through a thick cloud of foul coal-smoke, vomited forth in gigantic spirals from the chimneys of innumerable steamers. It is disappointing to contemplate for the first time the fairy city of Constantine as it were through darkly smoked glasses. Alas! the mysterious and meditative life of the East is no longer refractory to the hasty activity of the West. So-called barbarism is vanishing, and with it are vanishing the splendors of a world which was more concerned with beauty than with convenience. However, by a slight effort of imagination, one can eliminate the smoke, the shrieking steam-whistles, and a few hideous barrack-like buildings dotted here and there on the hills, and

then Constantinople appears before us so beautiful and so brilliant that we can hardly believe it
to be real. It seems more like a magnificent
scene painted by some Titanic artist for a theatre
of Babylonian immensity. And this first impression is exact, in a way, for closer acquaintance
will show that Constantinople is a city of apparent and ephemeral gorgeousness, which one feels
may some day suddenly disappear at the signal
of a mighty and unknown scene-shifter.

Before the anchor was cast, the *Ceres* was surrounded by caïques and small boats of all kinds,
and picturesque-looking watermen and hotel touts
offered their services in all the languages of the
earth ; shouting each other down, and bewildering the stranger with the babel of their voices.
Finally we stopped in mid-stream ; with a crash
and a whirr the anchor fell, and in a second the
deck swarmed with porters, who had scaled the
sides of the ship without waiting for the compan-
ion ladders to be lowered. Under the guidance
of the tout of the Hôtel d'Angleterre I was conducted ashore, and, having an absolute minimum
of luggage, I faced the custom-house officers bold-
ly, laid my valise on the muddy pavement, showed
them my spotless linen and my inoffensive change
of shoes, and assured them that I had no books.
The Turkish authorities are peculiarly keen in
searching for books, which they generally seize
and send to the censorship for examination ; and

the censor, if he does not confiscate them, tears out or obliterates any remarks they may contain disparaging to Turkey or to Turkish institutions. Even the Divine Comedy is prohibited in the Sultan's dominions, because Dante has spoken in unflattering terms of Mahomet. I may observe, once for all, that the Turks seem to do all in their power to discourage travellers from visiting their country, while Turkish officials of all classes look upon the foreigner as legitimate prey, and upon *bagchich* as a sure source of revenue, which Providence has given them to compensate for the irregularity of the payments of their empty national treasury. Travelling, like life itself, is a perpetual sacrifice ; but one soon gets accustomed to its inconveniences and irritating extortions, even in Turkey, where they pass all measure. It is useless to grumble. At a French watering-place where I once spent the summer, there was among the visitors a portly gentleman, who was always complaining of the accommodation, of the cooking, of the service, of everything. "From what you say, monsieur," said the head-waiter to him one day, "you must live very comfortably in your own home, and your domestic arrangements must be perfection." "Mon Dieu! yes," answered the murmuring guest, unsuspectingly. "Then why do you come to live here?" asked the waiter. Evidently, one does not go travelling over the face of the earth in search of the comforts of home, and therefore I shall beg leave to say no more about the discomforts of Constantinople.

Delivered from the hands of the custom-house officers, I followed my guide through the narrow and tortuous streets of Galata; ascended the heights of Péra by the tunnel railway; demanded hospitality at the Hôtel d'Angleterre—one of the dearest and most comfortless inns I have yet discovered; and, after a sort of breakfast, I started out to explore the city, taking with me a long-legged and intelligent guide, whose name was Perikles, and whose services were most valuable. The foreigner who speaks neither Greek nor Turkish cannot well dispense with a guide.

Péra is the Frankish quarter of Constantinople, —a long, narrow, irregular street, lined with European shops, and traversed along the upper part by a tramway. Yes, there is a tramway at Constantinople. Alas! there are tramways everywhere, nowadays, even at Bagdad, the capital of the Caliph Abdallah Haroun Alraschid. There are European cafés in the Grand Rue de Péra, and Tauchnitz editions in the windows of the bookstores. It is a mongrel, cosmopolitan quarter, comparatively clean, well-built, and uninteresting. Let us away, Perikles, and over the water to old Stamboul.

No; not by the tunnel. Enough of steam and progress and Western civilization. On foot we will go; and, first of all, to the Petit Champ, to the old Turkish cemetery, part of which has been converted into a public garden. A little way up Péra Street, turn to the left, and here we are on the brow of the hill that slopes down from Péra to the Golden Horn, and before us is Stambóul, with its mosques and minarets. At our feet the slope is dotted with sable cypress-trees and marble stakes surmounted by turbans, on which may still be seen traces of color. These stakes, which are tombstones, lean at all angles — some to the right, some to the left—while others lie flat on the ground, half buried and broken in fragments by their fall. This cemetery has long been abandoned by the Mussulmans, who will not bury their dead in such close vicinity to the Giaours; and gradually the living are reconquering the territory, and wooden houses and gardens are springing up on the hillside, and roads traverse the field of the dead; and behold the inevitable tramway clattering along under the shade of the funereal cypresses !

Beyond this foreground of cypresses and tombstones, we see the brown roofs and red houses of the quarter of Kassim Pacha; beyond this belt of habitations are the blue waters of the Golden Horn —that long gulf which stretches from the Bosphorus up to the Sweet Waters of Europe; while the background of the picture is occupied by the amphitheatre of undulating hills on whose slopes Stamboul is built. Beneath the pure blue sky and in the clear white light of the morning sun, the magnificent line of the horizon extends from the Seven Towers to the heights of Eyoub, varied by the brown domes of the bazaars and baths, the white minarets of the mosques, the arches of the old aqueduct of Valens, the tufts of cypress and plane trees that spring here and there from amid the rose and blue masses of the roofs, and, at the extremities, by the suburban houses, whose smiling gardens embroider the old ramparts of the Palæologi. To the extreme left is the palace of Seraï-Bournou, with its white battlemented walls, its trellised kiosks, its shady gardens; the mosque of Sultan Achmet, with its majestic cupo·la guarded by six snow-white minarets; Saint Sophia resting its dome heavily on its solid props of confused masonry, surmounted by four minarets; the mosque of Bayezid, with its fluttering canopy of pigeons. Then come the Yeni-Djami, the buildings of the War Department, and the immense column of the Seraskier tower, from whose summit the watchman scans the combustible city day and night, to signal the smoke of the commencing fires. To the right is the Arabian finesse and elegance of the Suleimanich, and other minor mosques, which rise with lesser splendor, towards Balata. And all this panorama is reflected in the silvery mirror of the Golden Horn, and seems to be painted with the colors of a dream—roseate, opaline, lustred, delicate, and caressing, like the colors of orchids, those dream-flowers. It is true, the marvellous picture requires certain conditions of light and perspective; and we have only to cross the bridge, to climb those tortuous and narrow streets, and to come close to those fragile palaces, in order to convince ourselves that the splendor of Constantinople is as unreal as the splendor of the architectural fictions of the scene-painter. Nevertheless, the fact of our having been admitted to the dusty coulisses does not authorize us to deny the sublimity of the spectacle.

II.

To reach Stamboul, you cross the bridge of boats which stretches over the Golden Horn from Top-hané to the other side. To approach this bridge, you pass through the commercial quarter of Gala-ta, where there are shops that remind one of the shops in the Bowery at New York, a Bourse, and a profusion of money-changers' stalls, where you change your good gold for heavy silver *medijiehs* and dirty *paras*, whose base alloy is stamped with decorative Turkish characters. All over the city the money-changers have their tables, which they set up in doorways and at street-corners, like the Auvergnats, who sell roasted chestnuts, and ensconce their portable ovens under the *portes-cochères* of Paris. The word "table," although consecrated by Scripture, is not quite exact, for these tables are in the shape of glass show-cases, in which are displayed, safe from the grasp of too nimble fingers, the various currencies of the Levant and of all the other countries of the earth, intermingled often with jewelled arms, precious stones, or gold ornaments.

After paying a *para* to one of the toll-keepers who stand at the entrance of the bridge, we found ourselves in a new atmosphere. While passing through the narrow streets of Galata, I had been so deafened and bewildered by the noise and movement that I had gathered nothing but a confused impression of a motley crowd of men and dogs and vehicles, and of a babel of sounds, above which rose the shrill cries of the street-venders and the repetition of the warning *guarda*, uttered by the muleteers and drivers. On the bridge— which is built of roughly hewn beams laid crosswise, worn by tramping hoofs into cavities and ruts, and always under repair—pack-horses, mules, asses, carriages, and bullock-carts jolt and rumble along; from time to time the stylish coupé of some pacha or high official dashes past, with the clatter of a discharge of artillery; amid the vehicles and on the sidewalks, there is a constant going to and fro of representatives of all the nations of the earth, clad in all the costumes of the East and of the West; on each side the bridge are the landing-stages for the local steamers which ply up and down the Golden Horn and along the Bosphorus; darting in and out, under the bridge, are caïques and row-boats; and all around, which-ever way we look, are mosques and minarets and domes — the panorama of Constantinople, the white fairy seated in calm majesty on her throne of seven hills.

Leaving the bridge, and crossing the market on the quay, radiant with pyramids of watermelons, we arrive at Stamboul: *eis ten polin*, as the Greeks used to say; Istamboul, as the Turkish ear caught the sounds. Now, first of all, good Perikles, guide me to the bezestin, to the khans, to the bazaar, so that I may see in what conditions the Sultan of Casgar's purveyor sold his rich stuffs to the favorite Zobeide, in the days of the Caliph Haroun Alraschid.

"But Haroun Alraschid lived at Bagdad, *kurie*," objects Perikles.

"Bagdad, Damascus, Balsora, the island of the Old Man of the Sea — the place matters little; all over the East the bezestin is similar. Lead on, Perikles! Are not these men in tall black fezzes Persian merchants? Is not the first bazaar we shall come to the Egyptian bezestin?"

In a few minutes we enter an immense gallery, which at first seems almost dark in comparison with the bright light of the street which we have just left. Is it a gallery or a tunnel? Straight ahead the obscurity grows more opaque, until the eye distinguishes, in the far distance, a luminous patch, the exit at the other end of the gallery. The pavement, laid centuries ago, and sloping gently towards a central gutter, is composed of irregular stones, separated by interstices of varying dimensions ; indeed, sometimes the interstices dominate, and the stones have disappeared. Then, on each side are the stalls of the merchants, and the merchandise displayed in heaps or in open sacks— henné, sandal-wood, cinnamon, ambergris, benzoin, mastic, opium, hachich, sulphur, ginger, antimony, powder of aloes, and mountains of aromatic drugs, which exhale a penetrating exotic odor that seems to stupefy the grave merchants, who sit, dreamy and motionless, awaiting the customer's call.

At the end of this gloomy gallery a lateral alley is devoted to the cotton market, and there the activity appears greater, and operations of weighing and bargaining are going on.

We continue our route through a narrow street, occupied by the copper and tin smiths, who are manufacturing pots and pans with a deafening clatter of hammers ; and so we enter the grand bazaar. This name must not mislead the reader. The exterior aspect of the great bezestin has nothing monumental ; the brownish-gray blank walls, without windows, are surmounted by flattened domes, and attached to these walls, like lichens and fungi around the trunk of a tree, are innumerable sheds, and stalls, and parasitic structures, occupied by minor industries.

3

The bazaar covers an immense tract of ground, and forms a sort of subterranean town within a town, having its streets, and squares, and cross-roads, and fountains, its restaurants and bath-houses, surmounted by cupolas, where men and women go at all hours of the day to submit their bodies to the delights of massage and shampooing; the whole composing a labyrinth of sombre galleries, where a stranger can with difficulty find his way, even after many visits. The streets are long, vaulted passages, and the light falls from the roof through windows reserved in the summits of those little cupolas which we saw from the Péra heights—a soft, vague, and suspicious light, more favorable to the seller than to the buyer. The walls and ceilings of these lofty galleries are white-washed or tinted, and relieved with garish ornaments in blue or red; and on each side are stalls; and behind the stalls are inner shops, where the more precious objects are kept. In this gallery are piles of gaudy Manchester cotton goods and all kinds of mercery; other galleries are devoted to shoe-shops; in others are arms, silks from Broussa, Indian and Persian cashmeres, dolmans stiff with gold embroidery, caftans, gandourahs, and other vestments of exquisite colors; in another gallery are the sellers of rose-water, cosmetics, perfumes, chaplets of amber, jade, ivory, and fruit-stones; here are the spinners of gold and silver thread for embroidering slippers, tunics, cushions, and uniforms. Ignoring or disdaining machines, the spinners sit barefooted, and, with the ends of the strands attached to their big toe, they twist delicate cords of supple metal, as they smoke interminably cigarettes of perfumed tobacco. Here, in a bare and cold-looking gallery, are the diamond merchants and dealers in precious stones, who hide in their miserable stalls incredible riches, over which they keep watch, like the others, smoking cigarettes or nargilehs. And all day long the bazaar seems to be full of people. The dealers are Turks, Jews, Armenians, Persians, Greeks; the buyers are of equally miscellaneous nationality; and amid the crowd, rendered so picturesque by the variety and color of the costumes, there circulate itinerant venders of fruit, of water, of bread and cheese, of *kebabs*, and of sweet cakes and bread-rings sprinkled over with crushed almonds. Here and there you come to a little café, where groups of men may be seen sitting cross-legged, and pulling away at hubble-bubbles. There, through an open door, you get a glimpse of the first chamber of a bath-house, where you see men with shaven crowns standing about wrapped in white *peignoirs*, or lounging on divans. Suddenly you hear a horrible sound of monotonous and piercing howling, and a tall figure, clad in rags, is seen towering above the crowd. It is a blind beggar, who, with his palms held open behind his ears, is shrieking at the top of his

voice, or, as he would say, singing. During my
stay in Constantinople my favorite amusement of
an afternoon was to go over to Stamboul, accept
the kind invitation of some merchant to take coffee in his shop, and sit there for an hour, gossiping and watching the movement of the bezestin.
Such an invitation may be readily accepted, and
you may even inspect a merchant's whole stock
without buying anything, and yet he will not
grudge you his hospitality and the savory cup of
coffee. It is not the splendor of the bazaar that
strikes one ; indeed, as we have seen, the bazaar
is a dirty, ill-lighted, and cheap-looking place. It
is not the aspect of multifarious merchandise—
rich stuffs, and all the fabulous luxury of the
East—for, after all, there is little but paltry and
current goods in the bazaar nowadays, and our
Western dealers, and even such establishments
as the Louvre, the Bon Marché, and the other
grand bazaars of London and Paris, can boast
a finer stock of stuffs, carpets, and Oriental arms
than any of the dealers of Constantinople. The
routes of commerce have changed, and the traveller who goes to Stamboul thinking to come back
laden with treasures is doomed to disappointment.
If he does happen to find something exceptional,
he will inevitably pay dearer for it than he would
pay in other parts of Europe ; and that, too, after
having had to go through the disagreeable process of bargaining and beating down, which is the

beginning and end of Oriental ideas of business. My experience in the bezestin revealed to me the fact that, as a rule, the dealers ask for any object, even for a pair of *babouches*, just five times the price they are willing to accept. Nor did they ask me this price because I was a Frank and a Giaour, but because such is their habit, whether they are dealing with Franks, or Mussulmans, or Zoroastrians. No; to my mind the interest of the bazaar is in the general aspect. The bazaar forms a sort of neutral ground, where you can observe the Turk, and the Persian, and all the other people who meet there, without their resenting your curiosity; it is a place where curiosity is legitimate, and where everybody indulges freely in the satisfaction of that sentiment. Above all, the bazaar is an Oriental institution, which has remained unchanged except in the character of the goods sold. It is true, one sees there bales of Manchester cottons, rolls of English cloth, cargoes of Russian hollow-ware; but this fact does not prevent one seeing at every moment details of life and customs which are precisely noted in that inimitable mixture of fancy and realism, the stories of Scheherazade. It is a perpetual charm to the eyes to see this living exhibition of costume; to note here a dervish, there a turbaned Turk who has made the pilgrimage to Mecca, there a grave Persian, and there a swarthy eunuch who cannot find diamonds big enough for his vanity. It is amusing, too, to watch the coquettish ladies of the middle classes, who come in groups of two or three, followed by their children and their negresses, the latter carrying big bags, into which their mistresses pass their purchases. For, although Moslem jealousy does not allow women to keep shop, and although in the whole quarter of Stamboul you will not see a single woman of any nationality engaged in commercial occupations, there are no more active buyers and no keener bargainers than the Turkish ladies. Draped in their long *feridjis*, and with their faces and heads enveloped in the white *yachmach*, they spend hours and hours in the bazaars, chattering like magpies, and lavishing torrents of abuse on the "dog of a Christian," on the "son of a father who is roasting in hell," on the Giaour who dares to look too fixedly into their beautiful, flashing eyes. Sometimes, also, but then under the guard of a eunuch, you see in the bazaar women of higher rank — perfumed flowers of the harem, whose white and delicate visages the sun has never tarnished, but who, like their less favored sisters, seem to dream only of dress and sugar-plums.

I confess that this contempt of the Franks, which the Turks do not disguise, gave me much pleasure. They at least, among all the nations of the earth, have not bowed the knee before the idol of progress. Firm in the faith of their fathers, they calmly ignore Western civilization ; and if they do recognize the existence of the Occidental, it is only to despise him, and not to ape him and thereby lose their own personality, which has been the fate of so many nations who have become the victims of Western propagandism and Western ideas. At Constantinople, or, at least, in Stamboul, you feel that you, a Frank, do not exist in the eyes of the Turk. You may wear the largest check suit that a London tailor can produce, and yet the Turk will pass without deigning even to look at you. At the public fountains he will go through all his religious ablutions in your presence as if you were miles away. He will spread out his carpet, turn his face towards Mecca, and say his prayers while you are looking on ; and so mean are you in his estimation that he ignores you. For this dignity and stability of character I respect the Turk ; and I am grateful to him for procuring me a sensation which is not common in foreign travel, in Europe at any rate —the sensation that I am an intruder, a contemptible dog, a person worthy only to be spat upon and killed. Happily, the diplomatic relations which the Sublime Porte still entertains with the Western world guarantee the material security of the traveller in the Sultan's dominions. But everything in Constantinople tells us that the Turk, although he has now been living in Europe for centuries, is still a nomad in nature and a conqueror by inclination. In Constantinople the Turks camp rather than dwell, and were they to be driven out of the city to-morrow, they would leave behind them no monument of their genius but tottering tombstones and tumble-down wooden houses.

III.

Anything comparable to the paltriness and filth of the streets of Stamboul it would be difficult to find; and yet nothing can be more interesting than a ramble in the maze of narrow alleys which branch out in all directions around the bezestin, and cover the slope, which is crowned by the Seraskier tower, with a close network of humble but busy workshops. In these streets you are always going up-hill or down-hill; the pavement is of indescribable irregularity, and at every few yards' distance it sinks, and in the hole thus formed you find a litter of puppies, on which you must beware of treading unless you wish to provoke the anger of the mother; in the middle of the road, in the gutter, along the narrow curb-stone, in the sun, in the shade, everywhere and at every turn, you see scores of yellow, mangy, wounded, and mutilated dogs — some with three legs, some minus their nose, some with their ears torn into fringe, all scored over with scars—who go foraging about, or lie in the sun wherever they please, undisturbed by any one. At Constantinople the men get out of the way of the dogs, and not the dogs out of the way of the men. Nay, more : at Péra, and in the lower part of Stamboul, where there is a tramway, I have seen a car stop, and heard the driver use, not the lash, but soft and persuasive words, in order to induce a mangy cur to remove his hind-quarters from the rail across which he lay dozing in the sun. But in the labyrinthine streets on the slope of Stamboul, and, in fact, in most of the streets on that side of the water, carriages, and much more tramcars, are impossible, so narrow and so steep is the roadway ; and so, if you cannot walk, you must ride on a horse, while the owner of the horse runs behind. But the observer will prefer to walk, and, with the aid of extra thick boots, you can brave the pitiless pavement and perambulate with some ease. Then you will find yourself wending your way amid crowds of men, women, and children, ascending and descending, elbowed by a throng of hawkers bellowing out their wares, and roughly pushed to the wall by the leader of a string of pack-horses, which clatter steadily along, laden with sacks of flour, bundles of firewood, and every imaginable burden. On each side are little cafés, and money-changers, and water-sellers, who attract attention by an hydraulic mechanism which causes a clapper to revolve and clink against a number of glasses placed in a ring around it. At every ten steps you find sellers of grapes, and cakes, and sweets, and restaurants where the savory kebabs—little cubes of mutton interfoliated with bay leaves *à la brochette*—are seen roasting at the open window, on perpendicular spits, before a fire of charcoal contained in a narrow, upright iron basket. The Turk, it may be remarked, if not a great eater, is a perpetual eater, and all day long he is nibbling something, if he is not smoking or playing with the chaplet of beads which not only the Turks, but all the Levantine peoples, seem to carry as a plaything and a countenance-giver. As for the shops, in these streets in the vicinity of the bazaars they go by quarters; in one quarter, the narrow streets, picturesquely arranged with trailing vines crossing overhead from side to side, are occupied by butcher-shops; in other streets are cobblers, in others tailors, in others the makers of pipe-stems of cherry-wood or jasmine, in others the turners of amber, in others the coopers. And all these industries are practised with biblical simplicity and in the most primitive manner, *coram populo* and *en famille.* You see the father and the son working side by side at the front of the open stall; at the back, in the luminous shadow, are the objects already finished; on the floor, amid the refuse, a family of cats is playing; at the door reclines a wolfish-looking street dog; while, as they pass, the neighbors stop to talk, and take their leave with the name of Allah on their lips. In every street the picture is, in general outlines, the same. At Stamboul you feel that you are really in the East, and that all you see is characteristic of the East, and of the East unimproved and unexpurgated, in all its splendor of color, its brilliant sunlight, its primitiveness, its dirt, and its perfidy. My experience showed me that the sooner the visitor has done with the few obligatory sights of Constantinople the better; for the ordinary traveller the beginning and the end of Constantinople are the streets, the people, the life, the details of manners, the general aspect, the marvellous panorama of the city seen from afar.

IV.

It is not my intention, in these pages, to write a guide or *vade mecum* for the visitor to Constantinople, or even to relate all that I saw there, but rather to sum up the impressions which I received most strongly, and the impressions which I should seek to renew on the occasion of any future visit. To speak frankly, I found most of the special sights, curiosities, and monuments mentioned in the guide-books of very slight interest. This was, of course, not the case with the mosque of Saint Sophia. I had heard and read so much about this famous monument that even when I had reached the entrance, one morning, I hesitated before going in, and rested at a café under the trees opposite, and smoked a nargileh, in order to compose my thoughts and calm my nerves before taking this long-anticipated joy. While sitting at this café, on a low rush stool, with my cup of coffee on a similar stool, and my nargileh on the floor, I saw a sight which threw some light on the relative cleanliness of the foul streets of Constantinople, in spite of the absence of scavengers and drains. The café was under a sort of arcade, raised about three feet from the level of the square, and from this shady vantage-point I was watching the movement of the place : the fruiterers plunging their knives into the roseate flesh of watermelons, and offering for sale strange forms of gourds and colocynths; the open-air cafés under the trees, with their picturesque groups of smokers and talkers ; the barbers oper-ating in the open air, and thus affording the stranger the only occasion he has of seeing the cranial conformation of the Mussulman ; while in front of me stood the white and silent mosque of Saint Sophia, with its dome and its minarets ris-ing heavily from amid a green girdle of ancient plane-trees and sycamores. My immediate at-tention had been attracted for the moment by the picturesque figure of a young dervish, wearing a conical cap of gray felt, who stood near the en-trance of the mosque and counted his beads with sanctimonious air, when, just in front of the arcade where I was sitting, I heard a thud and a crash of pottery. It was a menial who had deposited a heap of refuse in the gutter. Now, a donkey, with panniers on his back, which happened to be standing hard by, spied this heap, approached and smelt it, and picked out of it some rinds of watermelons and other fragments of green stuff; then came a street dog, who found something to his liking; then followed a cat, who also found something; next a flock of pigeons alighted and devoured the watermelon seeds; and when the pigeons left the heap, there remained nothing but a fragment of broken crockery and a patch of moisture on the ground, which the sun dried up immediately. Thus in less than five minutes the whole heap of refuse, except the fragment of crockery, which would become amalgamated with the pavement, disappeared, without the intervention of brooms, or dust-carts, or any other costly applications of hygienic science.

But it is time to return to Saint Sophia. The exterior of this famous mosque is an absolute deception; the dome seems flat, the minarets have not the elegance of the Persian and Arab minarets, and the mosque itself is so encumbered with parasitical buildings — schools, baths, shops, and storerooms — that one cannot distinguish its real form. The interior, on the contrary, is grand, but grand by reason of its vastness, its proportions, and its form and lines alone, for all the rest is ruin and desecration: the mosaics of the dome have disappeared beneath a coat of whitewash;

the mosaics of the lateral arcades exist only in patches; all the ornamentation and all the movable splendor of the church can scarcely be said to exist any longer, except in souvenir. Ah! when we appeal to the souvenir of history, and consider the Saint Sophia of the present day from that point of view, there are volumes to be written about it, in addition to the volumes which it has already inspired. On the bronze entrance door we can still distinguish the trace of the Greek cross; in the lateral gallery an incised inscription marks the traditional spot where the Empress Theodora sat to worship; at the end of the sanctuary, beneath the whitewash, we can follow vaguely the outline of a colossal figure of divine Wisdom, or rather holy Wisdom — Agia Sophia, the patron saint of the church; those pillars of gigantic girth and those enormous lustral urns were taken from the temple of Diana at Ephesus, from the temple of the Sun at Palmyra, and from the ruins of ancient Pergamos. And, as we contemplate these venerable and gigantic relics of the past, memory carries us back to Justinian and his empress, while at the same time an examination of the mosque throws light upon many questions which wanderings in Spain and elsewhere have suggested.

The Slav Oupravda, who took the name of Justinian, and was sole ruler of the Byzantine Empire for forty years (A. D. 527–565), may have adopted a mistaken general policy, as historians now maintain; but there is one merit which cannot be denied him—that of having been an active patron of art. Justinian was a great builder, and his chronicler and calumniator, Procopius, has devoted a special treatise to an account of the buildings raised by order of the emperor. Happily, we are not reduced to the text of Procopius alone; many of the monuments of the epoch of Justinian exist still, and among these the most celebrated is Saint Sophia, which, both in architecture and in decoration, was the type *par excellence* of Byzantine art, and became in turn a constructive type for Persian and Arab religious architecture. On the other hand, in the history of Christian art there exists no church of greater importance than Saint Sophia. Notre Dame at Paris had rivals, even in the neighboring provinces; St. Peter's at Rome is wanting in originality, and is Christian in little more than its destination; St. Sophia, on the contrary, has the double advantage of marking the evolution of a new style, and of attaining at once proportions which have never been exceeded in the East.

From the time of Constantine there had existed on the present site a temple in honor of Agia Sophia, which had been twice burned down when Justinian resolved to rebuild it in such a manner that it would surpass in splendor all that had been reported about the most celebrated edifices of antiquity, and in particular about the temple of Solomon. The richest materials, gold, silver, ivory, and precious stones, were employed with incredible profusion; enormous sums were spent, and new taxes and arbitrary measures had to be imposed in order to continue the works; furthermore, Justinian wrote to his functionaries and governors to send him materials already fashioned, and the governors accordingly pillaged the monuments of pagan antiquity. The prætor Constantine sent from Ephesus eight columns of verd-antique; other columns arrived from the Troad, the Cyclades, and Athens; Marcia, a Roman widow, sent eight columns of porphyry taken from the temple of the Sun. This fact explains the great diversity of stone and marble of all colors, which is so remarkable in this wonderful church.

The two chief architects were Anthemius of Tralles and Isidore of Miletus, who, it will be remarked, both come from those Asiatic provinces where architecture flourished with so much originality in the fourth and fifth centuries, as has been recently shown by the explorations of M. de Vogüé in Syria. M. de Vogüé has found the cupola and spherical vaultings, the dome supported by pendentives, in these Syrian ruins, dating as far back as the third century. But the architects who constructed these monuments seem only to have reproduced forms used centuries before in the antique edifices of Nineveh and Babylon. Recent researches, and above all the very complete studies of M. Marcel Dieulafoy, the excavator of ancient Susa, would seem to show that Byzantine as well as Gothic architecture is to be traced back ultimately to the art of the Assyrians, the Medes, and the Persians, which was itself influenced by Greek art, as has been eloquently proved by the recent discoveries made by M. Dieulafoy at Susa. Whatever may be the history and origin of the dome supported by pendentives, it is clear that the architects of Saint Sophia sought new inspiration in Asiatic sources, and we are almost justified in regarding them as continuators of forgotten masters who raised millions of bricks in vaults and lofty domes over the heads of Sargon and Nebuchadnezzar. In future, it will not be permissible to declare broadly that the Arabian, the Persian, and the Moorish styles are derived directly from the Byzantine.

But did not Saint Sophia serve as a type for the Mussulman mosque? Yes, and yet not, perhaps, so absolutely as some have stated, but rather accidentally and by force of curious circumstances. The mosque, as is well known, differs from the pagan temple in certain main points, namely: it has no *cella*, from which a carefully concealed divinity communicated with the worshippers through the intermediary of a priest; nor does it contain any graven images of human

4

form, which might lead into idolatry ignorant persons gifted with a too-impressionable imagination. Mahomet intended that the mosque should be a place of meeting accessible unto all and a house of prayer, for prayer was imposed upon the faithful as the chiefest duty towards God. The first religious edifice of the Arabs—who before Mahomet scarcely knew how to build at all, being by nature nomads and dwellers in tents—was a simple rectangular court surrounded by covered galleries or porticoes, the walls and roofs of which were of wood. In this court was a sanctuary; in the middle of the central nave was the niche, or *mihrab*, in the direction of Mecca, and a *menber*, or pulpit; near the entrance door were high platforms, whence the priests summoned the faithful to prayer five times a day; the lateral hypostyle porticoes were reserved for rest and reflection. In building these primitive mosques, the Arabs, probably at the suggestion of Byzantine architects, utilized the pillars of the pagan temples which they destroyed. The finest specimen we have of this primitive mosque is that of Cordova, a forest or quincunx of 1200 monolithic columns, now reduced to 850, which supported the low roof. These pillars were taken from Roman buildings at Nîmes, Narbonne, and Seville, and from various temples at Carthage and other African towns; so true is it that the Moslem was the thief of antiquity, and that the materials of his edifices were rarely extracted by him from the quarry.

But in this primitive mosque, it will be remarked that the dome does not exist. It is not until the fourteenth century that the dome appears in Mussulman monuments, when Sultan Hassan sends his architects to Mesopotamia, whence they bring back the secret of the cupola, and build the mosque of Hassan at Cairo. Then, in the fifteenth century, Mahomet II. enters Saint Sophia, and is so struck with its splendor that he proclaims that it shall be in future the model of all Moslem temples, although in its grand lines it contains the forms of the cross—the enemy and rival of the crescent. And so strong has been the influence of this model that on the plans of all the fine mosques of Constantinople and of Cairo the interior pillars describe the branches of the Greek cross. As for the court in front of the mosques, it is simply a reproduction of the atrium of the old basilicas. The ablution fountains and the minarets alone betray the Mussulman sanctuary, and these are in truth very minor accessories. Thus it happens that if the Franks were to drive the Turks out of Constantinople to-morrow, the Christian priests could at once celebrate mass in all the mosques of Stamboul just as correctly and naturally as they could in the church of Saint Sophia, if it were restored to its original purpose.

In historical interest the mosque of Saint So-

phia is inexhaustible, and you return to it again
and again to receive that impression of massive
grandeur and imposing majesty which its gigantic pillars and its colossal dome convey. But after
all, it is not the ideal mosque of Stamboul.   There
are three others more perfect exteriorly and in-
teriorly, namely, the Suleimanieh, the mosque of
the Sultan Bayezid, and the mosque of the Sultan
Achmet, which has six minarets.   The latter is a
model of elegance.   While the dome of Saint Sophia rests directly on the walls of the building,
that of the Sultan Achmet's mosque is raised on
a sort of drum, and springs up majestically in
the midst of several minor cupolas and of its six
slender minarets encircled by balconies whose
ornamentation has the fineness and intricacy of
jewellers' work.   The mosque is preceded by a
courtyard, around which are columns, with black
and white capitals and bronze basements, forming a quadruple cloister or portico.   In the middle of the courtyard is a beautiful fountain, rich
with arabesques, and covered in with a cage of
golden trellis work to preserve the purity of the
lustral water.   White, silent, and scintillating in
the sunlight, the elegant silhouette and graceful
proportions of the mosque of Sultan Achmet
challenge comparison with the finest monuments
of Persian art.

You enter this mosque through a bronze door,
having of course previously shod your profane

feet with protecting babouches; and then you
are free to examine and admire. The first feature
that strikes you is four enormous pillars, which
might be compared to four fluted towers, and
which support the weight of the principal cupola.
The capitals of these pillars are carved into the
form of a mass of stalactites, a style of ornament
which may be observed in many fine Persian
monuments; and half-way up they are encircled
by a band covered with inscriptions in Turkish
characters. The strength and simplicity of these
four pillars, which at once explain to the eye the
constructive system of the building, give a striking impression of robust majesty and imperish-
able stability. *Sourates*, or verses from the Koran,
form bands of running ornament around the great
cupola, and the minor domes, and the cornices.
From the roof are suspended, to within eight or
ten feet of the ground, innumerable lustres, composed of glass cups full of tallow, set in a circular iron frame, and decorated with balls of crystal,
ostrich eggs, and silk tassels, as in Saint Sophia
and all the other mosques. The mihrab, which
designates the direction of Mecca — the niche
where rests the sacred book, the Koran, the "noble book taken from a prototype kept in heaven"
—is inlaid with lapis-lazuli, agate, and jasper.
Then there is the usual menber, surmounted by
a conical sound-board; the *mastachés*, or platforms supported by colonettes, where the muez-

zins and other clergy sit. As in all the mosques, the side aisles are encumbered with trunks and bales of merchandise, deposited by pious Mussulmans under divine safeguard; and, finally, the floor is covered with fine matting in summer and carpets in winter.

While I was lost in wonderment at the splendor of this mosque, several Moslems came in to pray, with the usual prostrations, and beard-stroking, and yawning. Two or three women also came to pray, clad in feridjis of brilliantly striped silks — rose and white, azure and white, yellow and red — and they, too, knelt on the matting, and bowed and touched the ground with their brows; and their little baby girls, with their fine eyes and white veils wrapped round their heads, stood patient and motionless beside them, not being yet old enough to pray, or perhaps not strong enough on their legs to prostrate themselves without irremediably losing their balance. Some of these little baby girls seemed as beautiful as fresh flowers, and reminded one of the fair dreams of rosy childhood which we find in the pictures of the French painter Diaz. Then, in odd corners of the mosque, were boys learning the Koran under the direction of old turbaned priests, and others learning all alone, squatting cross-legged, with the sacred book open before them on a reading-stand in the shape of an X. These queer little boys produced the monotonous

and melancholy sounds which alone re-echoed in
the vast silence of the mosque; and in the immensity of the place, dotted as they were here
and there, near the mihrab and the mastachés,
they looked like big black fungi that had sprung
up through the pale straw-colored matting. Huddled up into a sort of sphere with a flat base, these
boys, each one acting independently, would rock
themselves rapidly backwards and forwards, while
they read aloud, in a sharp, nasal voice, a verse
from the Koran. Then they would stop, look
round, remain silent for a minute or two, and then
begin rocking and reading again. Sometimes a
single voice would be heard, to which another
voice would seem to respond. Another time,
two or three voices would be heard together, and
the immense vaults would receive and reverberate
the sounds, which composed a kind of monotonous and shrill music; for the Koran is full of
rhythmic prose, similar to that of which we find
specimens in the Pentateuch and the Psalms.

In all the mosques the general aspect of things
is the same, so that there is no need to describe
any of the others. The visitor, however, must
not forget to visit the courtyard of the mosque of
Sultan Bayezid, and to buy a measure of millet
from the old Turk who stands in the cloister, in
the midst of a swarm of beggars. Cast the millet
on the pavement, and in a second you will see
thousands of pigeons descend from the domes,

the minarets, the roofs and cornices of the surrounding buildings, and flutter round you with a
whirlwind of wings, settle on your shoulder, and
feed out of your hand, like the pigeons of Saint
Mark's at Venice. At this mosque, which is near
the bazaars, the observer will notice many interesting details of life, for the mosque is the centre
around which all Moslem life gravitates. Under
the arcades of the mosque the homeless sleep,
undisturbed by the police, for they are the guests
of Allah; in the mosque the faithful pray, the
women dream, the sick come to be healed; around
the mosque are schools and baths and kitchens
where the poor find food—for in the East real
life is never separated from religious life.

V.

The Atmeidan, or Hippodrome, of Constantinople is little more than a bare site, which memory
and documents alone can once more cover with its
ancient splendor of monuments and artistic treasures. On this vast open space stand almost all
the relics of ancient Byzantium that remain above
ground, and these relics are three: the obelisk of
Theodosius, the serpentine column, and the mural
pyramid of Constantine Porphyrogenitus, which
was formerly covered with bas-reliefs and ornaments of gilt bronze, and was so magnificent that
the historians of the time compared it to that
wonder of the ancient world, the Colossus of

Rhodes. Now it is simply a shapeless pillar of crumbling stones. The serpentine column, formed of three serpents twisted rope-wise into a spiral shaft, has lost the triple head, on which used to rest, if tradition may be believed, the golden tripod which the grateful Greeks offered to Phœbus Apollo, who had helped them to defeat Xerxes at the battle of Platæa. Although one may have been warned by the narratives of travellers that it is impossible to form an idea of old Constantinople except from the descriptions of mediæval writers, one still feels violent disappointment at finding that the ancient city has so completely disappeared. What! this deserted waste is all that remains of the Hippodrome which was the centre of the popular life of New Rome? Was it really on this spot that the greatest events of Byzantine history were enacted? Was it here, *à propos* of a question of charioteers, that Justinian saw a tempest rise which might have overthrown his power and his dynasty, had it not been for the courage of the pantomime whom he had made his empress-wife? Was it here that Justinian, second of the name, made prisoner by his rebellious subjects, had his nose and ears cut off? Was it here that the same Justinian, triumphantly returned from exile, donned the purple and walked over the heads of his vanquished foes, while the inconstant mob cried out, "Thou shalt walk on the aspic and on the basilisk"? And where is the

Augustæon celebrated by the mediæval travellers—that famous Forum surrounded on four sides with porticoes enriched with statues, the spoils of ancient Greece? Where is the circular Forum of Constantine, peopled with statues of pagan divinities? Where is the porphyry column on the summit of which Apollo, ravished from his temple in Phrygian Heliopolis, his head crowned with golden rays, consented to be renamed, and to represent the person of the Christian founder of the city? Where is that imperial palace which was a town of itself, and from whose windows the autocrat could see his fleets sailing forth to the conquest of Italy, Asia, and Africa, and the vessels of his merchants entering the Golden Horn, laden with the rarest riches of distant lands? Where are those thousands of statues that were brought from the East and from the West, from Athens and from Sicily, from Chaldæa and from Antioch, from Crete and from Rhodes, to augment the splendor of the parade of the Byzantine emperor, who appeared in the eyes of men like a god upon the earth?

Alas! the chronicler Villehardouin will answer our questions only too completely. When the Latins arrived before Constantinople, in 1203, he says: "You must know that those who had never seen it looked at Constantinople very much; for they could not believe that it was possible for so rich a town to exist in all the world, when they saw those high walls and those rich towers which enclosed it all around, and those rich palaces and those lofty churches of which there were so many that it was incredible, and the length and the breadth of the town, which among all other towns was sovereign. And know that there was not a man of them so bold that his flesh did not shudder." But soon the disasters began, and a whole series of fires destroyed a part of the town. "The barons of the army were sad at this, and had great pity to see those fine churches and rich palaces fall and sink into ruins, and those grand commercial streets burn with ardent flames;" and at one time, "there were more houses burned than there are in the three greatest cities of the kingdom of France."

It was still worse when the Crusaders took possession of the town, pillaged the palaces, sacked the churches, and destroyed this city of cities, this imperial centre of a brilliant civilization. The Crusaders did their work of devastation so completely that, after their melancholy triumph, there was little left for the nomad Turks to destroy. Constantinople was a city of ruins, and now even these ruins have disappeared beneath the dust of ages, and there remains of old Constantinople nothing but an obelisk, a crumbling pillar, a broken column of twisted bronze, and below the surface a dry cistern built by Constantine, where some poor Jews and Armenians live like gnomes or kobolds, spinning silk in the subterranean obscurity of its icy vaults.

VI.

Travelling is truly perpetual sacrifice. One cannot see everything, nor, on the other hand, can one describe everything one sees. The bazaars, the mosques, the Hippodrome, the Seraglio, the Sultan's palaces, the Sweet Waters of Europe and of Asia, and all the other curiosities of modern Constantinople, are certainly interesting; but the real interest of them is inferior to the reputed interest, and therefore I return to my primitive and final impression, that the wisest thing for the visitor at Constantinople to do is to content himself with a rapid inspection of the monuments, and to spend most of his time in wandering about the streets, observing men and manners, and returning again and again to the marvellous panorama of the *ensemble* of the city, seen now from the Seraskier tower, now from the Galata tower, now from the heights of Eyoub, and now from Mount Boulghourou, on the Asiatic side of the Bosphorus. This excursion will enable him to visit Scutari and its cemetery, and to hear the howling dervishes officiate. As for the whirling dervishes, who perform at Constantinople, I consider them to be comparatively unattractive; their evolutions remind one of those of the Parisian *frotteurs*, who put brushes on their feet in order

to polish the waxed parquet floors. The turning
dervishes achieve absolutely the same result, only
they work barefooted.

One morning, as I was wending my way to the
steamer, I saw at Top-hané a cargo of young Circassian girls landed, under the charge of a dealer
in human flesh. These girls were clad in indescribable drapery; they were dirty; they were
thin and bony; and they did not seem to possess
any elements of beauty. In reply to my inquiries,
I was told that these girls would be kept six
months or so; washed, combed, anointed, and
fattened; and that then they would be ready to
enter a pacha's harem. This information was
consoling, and in accordance with the biblical account of Esther, and of the preliminary proceed-
ings of Hegai, the king's chamberlain, the keeper
of the women of Ahasuerus, who had many maidens gathered in his house, and who was expert in
all preparations for beautifying the flesh. Esther,
it will be remembered, was not presented to the
king until "after that she had been twelve months,
according to the manner of the women (for so were
the days of their purifications accomplished, to
wit, six months with oil of myrrh, and six months
with sweet odors, and with other things for the
purifying [beautifying] of women)." It was no
small satisfaction to me, in this skeptical and
progressist nineteenth century, to find that these
Circassian young ladies were about to be sub-

jected to processes of beautification which had received the approbation of such a respected authority as Hegai, the king's chamberlain; and accordingly I went on board the Kadi-Keui steamer in a good-humor, and with the feeling that the day's sight-seeing had begun auspiciously.

At the village of Kadi-Keui, always with the aid of Perikles, I hired a victoria, drawn by two scraggy ponies, and driven by an eagle-faced ruffian, clad in many-colored rags and wearing a red fez. And so I began to make acquaintance with the roads of Asia Minor, for we were now no longer on the European continent. The streets of Constantinople had hitherto appeared to me to have achieved the *summum* of foot-torturing badness, but they are smoothness itself in comparison with the roads on the Asiatic side of the Bosphorus, which seem to have been the scene of Titantic battles in the stone age, and still remain strewn with the boulders and pointed blocks which the giants flung at each other. However, the ponies trotted and galloped and walked, and the carriage bounded from boulder to boulder; and we went up and down, between gardens and wooden châlets with closely grated windows, through fertile valleys, across dusty wastes, past silent villages, until at last we reached a mountain-top, some seven hundred feet above the point from which we had started.

On the summit of this windy mountain, sitting

on low stools, under the welcome shade of a gnarled old cypress-tree, we rested and drank some coffee provided by an enterprising Turk, who keeps a refreshment shed for the accommodation of tourists. Then, having lighted a cigarette, I proceeded to contemplate at my ease the panorama of surpassing magnificence which was spread out before my eyes. To the left, in the valley, the caravan road to Bagdad wound along the solitary, houseless tract like a colossal yellow serpent, losing itself amidst the low hills that rose in tiers, one behind the other, until they vanished from sight in the blue haze of the distant perspective, or dwindled away into the sparkling wavelets of the Sea of Marmora. I could have wished to see a caravan trailing along this famous road : mules laden with *khourdjines* and *mafrechs*—those carpet sacks in which the Orientals stow their provisions and luggage—camels bearing bales of precious merchandise, merchants, pilgrims, drivers, and all the diverse elements of the picturesque procession. Unfortunately, it was the season of the summer heat, and not the moment for caravan travelling. There was no help for it, and so, with regret, I turned my eyes from this impressive spectacle of the calm and vast plains of Asia Minor, and admired the smiling landscape of the Bosphorus, with its water-side palaces and hill-climbing villages, zigzagging its way between the mountains towards the Black

Sea. Then, finally, I turned once more, and behold, the sea, and beyond the point of San Stefano, and then Stamboul with its mosques and minarets, and Balata, and Phanar, and Péra, and Galata—all the seven hills of the city, embroidered with mosques and palaces reflected by the crystal waters of the Golden Horn. And all this marvellous ensemble of Constantinople glistened in the brilliant sunlight, and the waters looked like green and silver glass, and the domes and minarets stood out like brilliant points in this colossal fairy jewel.

Descending from the Boulghourou mountain, we passed through clumps of tumble-down wooden Turkish houses and through clouds of dust, until we entered the Turkish burial-ground at Scutari, an interminable forest of immense cypress-trees and tombstones crowned with fezzes and turbans—a most neglected, lugubrious, and yet not desolate spot; for in the middle of the cemetery is a leper-house, on the borders are dwellings and cafés, and through the centre passes the high-road. On this road we met a whole colony of Roumelians, who were emigrating, with all their goods and chattels, and a curious sight it was. Imagine, in the midst of this cemetery, with its endless perspective of tombstones leaning at all angles, and of cypress-trees whose black foliage glistened like jet in the blazing sun, a bend in the road; and as we approached this bend, a tall peasant

appeared, stalking barefoot between the heads of
a yoke of white oxen harnessed to a low four-
wheeled wagon, under whose mouse-gray awning,
stretched over low wooden hoops, were huddled,
pell-mell, veiled women, babies, calves, crockery,
provisions, bird-cages, agricultural implements, carpets, and miscellaneous utensils of all kinds. And
this peasant, and this yoke of white oxen, and
this primitive wagon and its varied load, was followed by other peasants, other white oxen, and
other wagons to the number of one hundred and
thirty, gliding in Indian file, slowly and steadily,
through the cemetery. These poor emigrants,
who were leaving their settlements in order to escape from the persecution of the Bulgarians,
looked weary and sad, and as the wagons passed,
in the midday heat, not a word, not a sound, rose
from any of them. The women sat motionless
amidst their children and household goods; the
men guided the oxen by gentle touches with a
slender wand. It seemed almost like a phantom
procession gliding through a sombre corner of
dreamland.

When we reached the extremity of the cemetery, we dismissed our ramshackle carriage, and
entered the precincts of a café, in front of which
was a fountain and a fine trellis-work arbor,
grown over with vines and jasmine. Under
this trellis, on cushions laid on high benches, we
sat, cross-legged, in the centre of an admiring

5

and friendly ring of mangy, leprous, and flea-bitten dogs, on whose coats the vermin visibly abounded. Here we ordered coffee and hubble-bubbles, and rubbed elbows with a lazy, lounging, ragged set of young and old Turks, who were smoking their nargilehs, and, like ourselves, waiting for the howling dervishes to begin their exercises.

The house of these dervishes, a sort of monastery, stands near the café, at the end of the main street of Scutari. It is a wooden house, surrounded by a garden and by the private graveyard of the dervishes. In front is a little courtyard, shaded by trailing vines, with on the right an old well, and beside it a bench, where we rested and waited until the preliminary prayers were over, when the curtain of the entrance door was raised, and we Giaours were admitted to the sanctuary. This is a large, square room, with galleries on three sides, and one of these galleries is fenced in with fine lattice-work, and forms the seraglio where the Mohammedan women go to see without being seen. The remaining galleries are open to ordinary spectators. On the ground-floor, beneath the galleries, is a promenade, part of which is reserved for Turks and part for Franks; and this promenade is separated from the rest of the floor by a low balustrade, within which are the dervishes. The floor is smooth and waxed, and on it are strewn sheepskin rugs.

At one end, in the direction of Mecca, is a mihrab, above and on each side of which are hung
on the wall various emblems, inscriptions from
the Koran, skewers, chains, spikes, knives, dag-
gers, maces, prickly chains, and various instru-
ments of torture, with which the dervishes sometimes wound themselves on days of very frantic
enthusiasm. Under the balustrade of the galleries are hung large tambourines. The walls are
of a warm gray color; the ceiling and all the
woodwork are painted a pale, æsthetic green, and
picked out with threads of *café-au-lait.* Through
the open window the sun shines in; you see the
vines and fruit-trees waving in the breeze in the
garden. The general aspect of the room is gay
and charming, and above all it is delightfully
soft and delicate in tone.

At the moment when we Giaours were admitted, the chief dervish and fifteen other dervishes
were prostrated, with their heads on the ground
in the direction of the mihrab, and for nearly half
an hour they continued kneeling, praying, and
bowing, rocking to and fro, and reciting the Koran in a twanging, nasal tone. Their costume
was not uniform. The chief, the *iman,* wore an
ample black gown and a black turban rolled
round a drab fez, while his four acolytes wore
turbans and robes of different colors—carmine,
green, puce, yellow; the other dervishes wore a
white under-robe, a black caftan, and a black and

white cap in the form of a turban. From the point of view of a colorist, the effect of the groups was very pleasing.

After the prayers were finished, one of the acolytes, seated in the middle of the floor, put his right hand to his cheek, as if he were suffering from excruciating toothache, and howled forth a kind of litany, to which the dervishes, ranged in line, responded in unison, swaying their bodies to and fro more and more violently, and shouting, "Allah-hou! Allah-hou!" The swaying and howling continued thus for half an hour, until all the dervishes were in a violent perspiration. Then there was a pause, and a fat acolyte in a puce robe came and gave each dervish a white cotton skull-cap in exchange for his turban. Then the man with the toothache began to howl the litany once more, and the dervishes started a series of more violent gymnastic exercises. They stood up in a row, shoulder to shoulder, swayed their bodies towards the ground, then backwards, then to the right hand and then to the left, their heads swinging loosely, their eyes closed for the most part. This exercise in four movements grew more and more rapid as the ecstasy of the dervishes became more complete; the floor shook with the dull thud of their heels, as they executed all together the backward swing; from time to time, one of the spectators, hypnotized by the sound and the rhythmic movement, stepped into the enclosure and joined the ranks, and soon the incessant cry of "Allah-hou!" developed into a furious roar, exactly like the roaring of a cageful of hungry lions. During a whole hour these dervishes swayed and roared, producing sounds such as no other human lungs could produce, lurching and swinging their bodies in unison, till their thin faces became livid with ecstasy and sweat. The noise was literally terrifying; one expected the whole room to fall in under this horrible clamor, as the walls of Jericho fell at the sound of Israel's trumpets. The faces of the dervishes grew convulsed, epileptic, illuminated with strange smiles. An odor of perspiration, reminding one of the odor of a menagerie, filled the room. And meanwhile the iman, with his delicate, ascetic face, remained calm and impassible, his lips moving in silent prayer, his hands encouraging the enthusiasts with pious gestures. At the end of an hour's uninterrupted howling and gymnastics, the excitement of the dervishes was at its height. Every moment you expected to see one fall exhausted. But no; they continued to quicken their movements as their cries became hoarser and more inarticulate. Then children were brought in and laid on the floor, three or four at a time, side by side, and the iman walked over them. Then grown men threw themselves down on the floor, and the iman walked over them; and they arose and departed joyously, believing that this salutary imposition of feet would cure them of their ills. After that, babes were carried in, and the iman walked over their frail bodies, supported this time by two of his acolytes, in order to render the pressure light. Finally, at a sign from the iman, the dervishes ceased howling and swaying, and began to wipe their perspiring faces, while a final prayer was recited. Then all walked calmly to their rooms in the monastery, and the ceremony was over. I never saw a spectacle more savage, strange, and exciting, and I never saw faces more calm, dignified, and even majestically beautiful, than the faces of some of these howling dervishes of Scutari.

To those of patient temperament who can travel happily without the aid of express trains and sleeping-cars, I would recommend the approach to Holland and Belgium by a rather roundabout and unfrequented route *via* Lille. I am supposing, of course, that our traveller is starting from Paris. The advantage of this route is that it enables you to visit Lille and Ostend, and to traverse a curious transitional country which is no longer French and not yet Dutch—a country where the natives talk a *patois* of their own, drink a peculiar kind of sourish beer, and indulge in formidable house-cleaning and floor-scrubbing on Saturdays. For that matter there is no absolute necessity of justifying the choice of this route by demonstrating that it has any advantages whatever. I chose it simply because I wished to see the museum of Lille, and so one fine August morning I left Paris with a ticket for that town.

From Paris to Arras you pass through an undulating agricultural country of no particular interest. Arras, with its fortifications *à la Vauban* suggests memories of old battle pictures of the days of Louis XIV. Towards Douai the wind-mills begin to appear, and the vast plain of Lille is thickly studded with black mills and their whirling, dingy red sails. Lille is a very large and prosperous manufacturing town, a sort of French Manchester, and, with the exception of the Exchange—a brick-and-stone structure rich in caryatides, medallions, and garlands, begun under the Spanish domination in the middle of the seventeenth century—it boasts no monument that imperiously requires to be visited. What a blessing it is to be free to ramble about a town that has no sights, and to be able to loaf and to invite one's soul without feeling the Baedeker dancing in one's pocket and pulling one up short at every ten steps to explain the interest of unin-teresting buildings! How sharp are one's impres-sions of local details, of the shape of the curi-ous long wagons that clatter along the streets of Lille, of the sound of the tramway signals, of the fine old doorways and iron gates that adorn many of the houses, of the rarity of cafés and the cor-responding multiplicity of *estaminets* and little beer-shops full of heavy Flemish boors such as Teniers painted, how novel the walks along the Deule river and along the canals which skirt the town — canals filled with sluggish black water, crossed by quaint bridges, and crowded with heavy barges with dirty red or dun-colored sails.

One may almost imagine one's self already in Holland, especially when one hears the Lillois speaking their obscure Flemish dialect.

After a stroll through the town, the thing to do is to make straight for the picture-galleries in the Mairie. The Musée de Peinture of Lille is certainly the richest public collection in France after those of Paris. The Flemish and Dutch schools are represented most brilliantly by eight large compositions by Rubens and two fine portraits by Van Dyck, to say nothing of Jordaens and Teniers. The pictures of the modern French school are alone worth going to Lille to see, notably Courbet's famous "Après-dinée à Ornans" and Delacroix's "Medea killing her children," a splendid painting, as brilliant in color as the day it left the studio. Unfortunately, the same cannot be said of the Courbet, which is growing very dark, owing to the working out of the bitumen largely employed by that artist in his figure-subjects. Then there is a scene in the forest of Fontainebleau by Troyon; two of Carolus Duran's finest works, " L'Assassiné " and " La Dame au Chien ;" Jules Breton's " Plantation d'un Calvaire," representing a numerous procession of clergy and villagers carrying the image of Christ out of the church towards the wooden cross that is awaiting it in the churchyard, beyond which we see in the background the red-tiled roofs of the village ; Paul Baudry's " Supplice d'une Vestale ;"

J. F. Millet's "La Becquée," a delicious picture, representing a peasant mother feeding three little rosy-cheeked children, sitting in a row on a door-sill. Among the pictures of the old French school there are important works by Greuze, Prud'hon, and Arnold de Vuez, a native artist, whose works are to be seen only at Lille; and a number of curious historical portraits by Boilly, including his "Triumph of Marat." But, besides its nine hundred pictures, many of them of the very first importance, the museum of Lille possesses an incomparable treasure in the Wicar collection of drawings of the ancient and modern masters, comprising more than 1400 specimens, mostly by the Italian masters, and including sixty-eight drawings of Raphael, one of which is a study for the "School of Athens." Among the French work I recommend to the visitor's attention the excessively rare drawings by Boilly, some exquisite female heads by J. B. Augustin, the drawing by Decamps, representing a man hung, and the drawings by Corot and Millet. But the pearl of the Wicar gallery is the bust of a girl of sixteen or seventeen years of age executed in colored wax, a little less than life size, a marvel of delicate realism, and, in expression, the very ideal of virgin chastity. Fac-simile reproductions of varying merit have recently rendered this beautiful work accessible to quite modest purses, but the extreme delicacy and mysterious charm of the original are as much beyond the reach of imitation as the smiling face of Leonardo da Vinci's "Joconde," the more so as this bust has two or even three different expressions according to the angle at which it is viewed. The front view is that of a very young and very chaste face, full of melancholy and resignation. The profile, on the other hand, is gay and almost smiling. The *profil perdu*, again, with the fine rolling hair, the strong modelling of the nape of the neck and of the ears, is very firm and superb, and even a little *sauvage* in the French sense of the word. This mobility of expression cannot fail to strike the spectator; it is a quality that one cannot analyze, and it is, I imagine, a powerful element in the power of fascination which this charming portrait exercises over all who have ever seen it. The wax bust of Lille has its *culte* and its fervent adorers in both hemispheres.

It is a curious fact that nothing is known about the origin of this bust. Wicar, the founder of the Lille Museum, made no special mention of it in his will and left no note as to the way in which it came into his possession. In vain the critics have asked when and by whom the work was made? Its attribution to Raphael is entirely groundless; equally untenable is the hypothesis that the bust is a miraculously preserved specimen of Greek art of the time of Pericles. The most probable theory is that of M. Gonse, who holds the bust to be of Florentine origin, and either by the famous ceroplastic artist Orsino Benintendi or by Verrocchio, at any rate a work of the fifteenth century.

With the charming vision of the wax virgin head fresh and radiant in my mind I left Lille and resumed my journey towards the Low Countries, as old-fashioned folks used to say. The route from Lille to Ostend was rather wearisome; the train stopped almost every five minutes; still for some time I took an interest in the numerous canals and windmills, and in the gradual change of the vegetation, which becomes of a richer and darker green as the train proceeds. At Roubaix you are struck by the fact that all the houses have gambrel roofs—that is to say, roofs whose slope is broken in the middle and thence descends almost perpendicularly. The whole town, with its deep-red brick-and-tile structures, looks very charming, with the dark - green background of fields and trees illuminated by a golden sunset. At Mouscron, the frontier station, you can make comparative studies of languages by deciphering the polyglot inscriptions painted on the walls. At Courtrai you may remark the increasing use of dogs as beasts of draught, and then go to sleep until you reach Ostend, for there is absolutely nothing to see but cornfields, patches of beet-root, pasture land, bleaching-grounds, gambrel roofs, and an occasional windmill. The country is flat beyond all conception. In the whole distance from Paris to Ostend there is not a single tunnel.

Ostend I found to be a fairly civilized and inviting place, peculiarly favorable to inactivity of all kinds. The town is amusing and full of shops, the sand-beach immense, and the bathing excellent. Apart from the sea-bathing, the distractions of Ostend are promenading on the splendid esplanade of the Digue de la Mer from early morning until late at night; fishing with nets on the estacade, or pier—little square nets suspended from poles fixed at an angle to the pier, and wound up and down to and from the water by means of a little windlass; regattas; an occasional horse-race; fireworks; and the innumerable distractions offered by the Kursaal, which consist of instrumental concerts at least twice a day, an unceremonious and very jolly dance every evening, reading-rooms, music-rooms, a restaurant, a café, billiard-rooms, and interminable lounging and gossiping and gazing at the sea. With sunshine, agreeable company, good music, a good cigar, a comfortable chair, a good cup of coffee before him on a neat little table, the spectacle of his fellow-loungers, and beyond them of the sands and the ocean, what more can a holiday seeker desire?

I felt so relatively happy at Ostend that I made no haste to continue my journey, and stayed there several days, sunning myself and noting the peculiarities of holiday-making humanity. Ostend is much frequented by Germans of the less agreeable kind—fat, blonde, coarse German men with tow-colored hair parted behind, obtrusive, clumsy Germans who wear gold spectacles and a cross expression, and walk about, with the *Cologne Gazette* in their hands, emitting guttural cries and rumblings which corrugate the receptive tympanum and irritate the nerves. There is also a fair sprinkling of English, the men swaggering in white flannel trousers, and admiring the pretty ladies with the deprecatory and apologetic inflections of voice peculiar to the race, rarely enthusiastically declaring a girl to be positively nice, but qualifying their praise by an adverb "*rather* a nice girl." Belgians, of course, abound, *savez-vous*, and there is the usual contingent of cosmopolitan adventurers, gamblers, titled financiers, male phenomena in knickerbockers, lonely ladies accompanied by showy poodles most useful for breaking the ice and creating pretexts for conversation, and eccentric characters whom it would require a whole chapter to enumerate, such as a worthy citizen of Munich who was so anxious to make the most of his holiday, and so eager to get out of doors in the morning, that he used to comb his beard as he walked along the esplanade, his face still shining with soap.

But enough of this frivolous sea-side observation. Ostend is delightful. I am bent upon pleasure.　There is no reason why I should hurry, and yet, since I have set out with the purpose of visiting Holland, it may be well to begin to execute my project.　Such were my reflections one morning as I called for a railway guide and began to study maps with a view to finding out the whereabouts of Holland.　Geographical ignorance, I have remarked, greatly enhances the pleasure of travelling; it reserves innumerable surprises for the wanderer and conduces to a consciousness of extreme liberty and boundless serenity.　The traveller whose geographical knowledge is vague forms general projects but not fixed plans, and consequently he is never the slave of an itinerary; he is always free to take advantage of opportunities and to yield to caprices; his projects are so very elastic that they cannot be thwarted; he has no responsibility, no cares, no anxiety to ruffle his mind; he is simply going to a country whose name summons up in his mind, not topographical facts or distinct notions of longitude, latitude, boundaries, and frontiers, but merely notions of an accidental literary or artistic nature.　When I determined to make a trip through Holland, and when by dint of deep study of time-tables I finally discovered the way to reach that country, one of the thoughts uppermost in my mind was the prospect of seeing innumerable windmills.　In all the countries I had hitherto visited windmills are no longer held in high esteem. In France the few windmills that still exist look like colossal wounded birds beating the ground sadly with their wings. They no longer enjoy the confidence of opulent and influential millers, and the corn that they grind can only be a dark-colored inferior grain, destined to be eaten by the poor and the unfortunate. Their glory has departed; they are no longer triumphant, as they were when they first arrived with the Crusaders—at least, so says the legend—from the East, the country of all inventions; but still they seem to have something human about them, all fallen into dishonor as they are. A windmill always has its individuality and its peculiar aspect. See how constantly the Dutch painters make one of them to animate their landscapes. In the immense battle-pieces of Van der Meulen these wooden-winged giants seem to smile at those heroic combats, as it were at the struggles of pigmies; in Ruysdael's sunny solitudes the windmill often appears; and Hobbema places its eccentric contour in the golden dust of his woodland roads. Among the moderns, Jongkind, to whom the French impressionist school of painting owes so much, excels in planting the enormous arms of a windmill against the pale sky of his fantastic landscapes. The black or red sails turn dismally; the roof is torn and rent by the angry winds; the staircase is worn out by the use of ages; the giant groans with the groans of the vanquished, and the hour is fast approaching when its death-rattle will be smothered by the roar of machinery, and its ruined carcase delivered up to utilitarian flames. But in presence of the new steam-mills the painter's brush falls from his fingers in disgust, while the image of the old windmill will live forever in the works of the great masters, and the artists will forever lament the captive flight of its wings in the serenity of a broad horizon.

Happily, in Holland the windmill still holds its position in the landscape and in the industry of the country; it stands out against the horizon triumphantly, like a brilliant star, or, as at Rotterdam and Amsterdam, towers up on the top of a huge brick pediment, in the very midst of the town. The windmills and the canals are still the two chief characteristics of Dutch landscape.

The first Dutch town I visited was Rotterdam. Nowadays, thanks to railways and modern improvements, the approach to nearly all towns is spoiled. You enter Rotterdam on a higher level than the roofs of the houses, amid the usual maze of rail tracks, stacks of coal, and sooty, serpentine water-hose. The station and the people about it look modern and dirty and commonplace. The only thing that strikes and makes one feel that one is travelling in a foreign country are the inscriptions and advertisements written in that queer Dutch language, that seems

6

now a corruption of English, and now of German
—a language which one is constantly on the
point of understanding, but without ever quite
achieving that happy result. Once outside the
station the charm begins. First of all there is
the triumphant and monumental windmill in the
centre of the town, and then, wherever you turn,
you find yourself in a labyrinth of canals, crowded with ships and boats of all kinds, bordered
with trees and boulevards lined with lofty houses.
The city is different from anything that can be
seen elsewhere in Europe. It is a combination
of streets, quays, canals, and bridges, so complicated that you can hardly feel sure whether it is
a dockyard or a town, whether there is more land
than water, and more ships than houses ; for each
canal is crowded with ships of all sizes except in
the middle, where there remains a dark-green
channel, by which the boats pass in and out.
You are moving along with the tranquil crowd
of Dutchmen, with their serious air and their
broad, yellow faces—but faces of a yellow such
as you do not see elsewhere, the yellow of Par-
mesan cheese—with their blonde, reddish, or yellowish hair ; some of them beardless, others with
a fringe of hair around their faces, such as the
English call a Newgate frill ; and among them
women, with equally yellow faces, long teeth,
broad haunches, and formless bodies, by no
means reminding one of the robust beauties

which Rubens painted. The men in this crowd
are neither well-looking nor stalwart, but small
and lean; as for the women, they are almost invariably very plain, and not always so clean and
tidy as tradition reports. Suddenly there is a
halt; the crowd thickens, a balance-bridge rises
in the air, a ship or barge glides past; the toll-
taker swings a wooden shoe, attached to a rod
and line, and angles for the toll money; the
bridge falls into position again, and the crowds
and the carts pass on, calmly, seriously, as if they
were trying to show the observant stranger how
good they can be. Yet the streets of Rotterdam
are full of animation. Tramways run in every
direction, and there is a constant tinkling of their
bells to warn the innumerable carts to clear the
track. But all the movement is commercial;
you see very few carriages, no display of elegance, and very few showy shops. In fact, the
vast majority of the shops in the streets of Rotterdam are tobacco and cigar shops, silversmiths,
and provision stores. The profusion of shops
for the sale of eatables and household wares is
extraordinary. Evidently it is more profitable in
Rotterdam to appeal to the palate than to the
eye.

· With all their movement there is a singular
calm reigning in the streets of Rotterdam. The
faces of the passers-by are stolid; there is no
chattering, no gesticulating. The population is

imperturbably good. I was constantly struck by this feature of the Dutch wherever I went; they are preternaturally tranquil. At Rotterdam, it may be argued, the people are occupied with their business, and have no time to be gay and noisy. But at their holiday resorts they are equally quiet. One Sunday afternoon I went down to Schevening-en, the famous seaside resort, near the Hague, and I was utterly astounded at the bearing of the crowd of holiday-seekers. I could hardly help thinking that the whole thing must be a toy, and that the people were playing at being good. The hotels on the top of the sand-dunes, the neat, brick-paved, winding footpath that runs the whole length of the upper part of the beach, the villas, the casino, the village; the church, with its clock-dial painted red and blue, with the hours picked out in white; the little canvas bathing-machines, brilliant with new paint; the little tents on the beach, the fishing boats, all seemed to accord with this idea, they were so neat and proper. When we arrived, all the people were out on the beach; the Sunday holiday-makers, too, had arrived; and yet the tranquillity, the stillness, the absence of the sounds of gayety, or, indeed, of any human sounds, were so marked that it made one feel quite uneasy. You met groups walking quietly; here and there were groups sitting quiet-ly and talking quietly; and quiet smiles pervaded at rare intervals their buttery physiognomies. I presume these people were enjoying themselves in their own quiet way. But how unlike a Latin crowd at the seaside!

At Scheveningen I saw no more style, no more elegance, no more coquetry than at Rotterdam. Very few of the Dutch women wore their quaint native head-dress, and these few had surmounted it by horrible Parisian bonnets. As for their dress, it was horrible. Their hips were extravagantly bulged out with skirts, and their general appearance was painful to eyes heedful of grace of line. Once for all, I may say that, generally speaking, I found the Dutch women uncomely, the children unpleasing, and the men ugly, coarse, and unsympathetic. Dutch cleanliness is proverbial, I know; but, nevertheless, the Dutch are not a well-washed nation. In all their towns I found but poor washing appliances and a sad absence of bath-houses.

But let us leave the Dutch people, with their austere airs and their dismal black costume, and talk rather about their country, the most curious, the most charming, and the most *far-away* country one can find without going outside of Europe. What struck me most in the country itself were the color and the light and shade. It has been said that if all the visible testimonies of the existence of Holland in the last two centuries had disappeared, except the work of the Dutch painters, we should be able to form an idea of the whole country and of its life and manners in its pictures; the towns, the country, the ports, the canals, the markets, the shops, the costumes, the arms, the household utensils, the food, the pleasures, the linen, the religious beliefs, all the customs, manners, qualities, and defects of the people are expressed in its painting. And through seeing specimens of this painting in the museums of the world one becomes so familiar with every detail of Dutch life and landscape that when one does visit the country and sees the real thing, one is tempted to remark, naïvely, "How like a Dutch picture!" But none of these pictures, excellent and truthful though they are, can give a thoroughly adequate idea of the color and the effects of light and shade one sees everywhere in Holland. To see and appreciate that you must visit the country itself. You must travel through miles and miles of terrestrial platitude, where the horizon has no accidents except a windmill or a clump of trees; where the cottages are deep red, the meadows deep green, the sky gray-blue, capable of changing almost at any moment into the most curious shades of black-gray and burnished copper, torn up and shredded and twisted as if some aërial giant had amused himself by combing the clouds into a tangle. And these dark-green meadows are intersected by innumerable little canals filled with black water, and over the canals are black bridges and black gates, and in the

meadows are black cattle ; in the distance the inevitable but welcome windmill has black sails,
and even the rows of willows and poplars have a
black tinge in their green. And over this country the sun shines blazingly in high summer-time,
and, especially in the late afternoon, it sets off
vast spaces of golden light against other spaces
of that black, intense, bituminous shadow that
you see in the paintings of the Dutch school.

Then when you come into the town you find
rows of deep-red brick houses, with tile roofs of
all shades from black up to scarlet, with gables of
all imaginable shapes, and with an inclination
over the street at any angle except the angle of
the house next door. To look along the façade
of a quay at Rotterdam, for instance, you might
almost think that the city had been disturbed
by an earthquake, so curiously and irregularly do
the houses lean outwards. The front doors are
brilliant with brass name-plates and fittings ; the
sash windows are painted white and dressed with
white blinds, white curtains, flowers and plants
in pots, and outside these is an arrangement of
mirrors called *speis*, or spies, which enables the
people inside to see what is going on in the
street without themselves being seen. The façades of the streets of Rotterdam present but two
colors—dark red and white. Seen from a distance, the houses seem to be almost black, and
with the strong contrast of the white lines of the

windows and cornices they look quite funereal. On the other hand, when you examine them more closely, they assume a comical and carnivalesque aspect. Most of the houses have only a breadth of two windows and a height of two or three stories, but the façade rises above and conceals the roof, narrowing up into a truncated triangle, into depressed and interrupted arches, or, more commonly, the frontal is cut into steps like the toy houses that children build with wooden bricks. These frontals are bordered with a white cornice and often adorned with heavy ornaments and arabesques in relief, and in the middle a beam juts out with a pulley at the end to draw up baskets or weights. But all these houses are so clean, so spick and span, so neat, so miniature, and so comic in aspect that you can hardly believe that they are the dwellings of sober and worthy citizens, and not the back-scene of some comic opera or the paraphernalia of some immense carnival.

This impression that you are in a toyland constantly strikes you in the Dutch towns. Everything is so orderly, and so much care is given to details. The very trees that run in tall rows along the canals seem unreal, so dark is the green of their foliage, and so calm and sleepy their outline. The canals themselves, with their serried ranks of imprisoned ships, seem hardly practical. Surely these gayly painted barks cannot carry merchandise ; they cannot come from anywhere or go anywhere ; they cannot pass the innumerable bridges with their tall masts ; certainly they can only be toy boats placed there to fill up the scene! In reality nothing could be more serious than the Rotterdam canals and the Rotterdam boats. Along the quay of the Meuse, transatlantic steamers can be moored, and many of the canals in the heart of the town are so deep that sea-going ships can come up to them and unload their cargoes at the very warehouse doors. But most of the boats that you see on the Rotterdam canals navigate simply on the Rhine and the Dutch canals. These have only one or two masts ; they are broad, bulky, robust boats, tricked out with paint and varnish like gala barges. Many are painted green exteriorly, with broad bands of white or red running from end to end. The poop is gilded ; the deck, the masts, and the spars glisten with varnish. The deck-house, the hatches, the tips of the masts and spars, the water-barrel, the hen-coop, the chains, rings, and blocks are all painted with gay tints of red, green, or blue picked out with white. The house on board, where the skipper and his family live, is generally as gayly painted as a Chinese kiosk, and at the little windows the curtains are tied up with gay ribbons, and the flower-pots are painted bright red, and the brass curtain-rods are rubbed till they shine like mirrors.

Now, imagine the effect of all this mass of color, of this forest of masts and ropes and sails and streamers, set off against the dark background of the trees and houses and quays; in mid-canal imagine a little row-boat, laden with fruit and vegetables, standing out with their brilliant reds and greens and yellows against the black water of the canal; at the end of the canal picture the square cathedral tower and a vision of huge windmill sails, and overhead a sky full of sinister obscurations, changing and moving perpetually; add to this vision the human element—sombrely dressed men working tranquilly, little servant-maids with lilac dresses and quaint white head-dresses, perpetually occupied in scrubbing and sweeping and rubbing — and you will then have some idea of the superficial aspect of Rotterdam, the chief commercial city of Holland.

In going from Rotterdam to Delft I saw for the first time what Dutch landscape really is. We started one afternoon from the Delft Gate on a *stoomboot* unworthy of the name. It was a sort of barge, with cabins fore and aft and engine and smoke-stack amidships. The craft was painted green with white stripes. The roofs of the cab-ins were asphalted, and on the roof of the fore-cabin were placed folding X chairs; while on the roof of the aft, or second-class cabin, were placed queer, stubby little benches about six inches high. We wondered why the Dutchmen liked to sit so low, but, being strangers, we made no remarks. The start was uneventful. We took on board three pigs — much against their wills — an ice-cream machine with its roof and fixings, several hampers and baskets of fruit, a young Parisian married couple, Georges and Thérèse, and some odd native passengers. By means of poles and strenuous efforts the boat's head was got round, and we steamed forward. Remark that during the difficult operation of taking the pigs on board and turning the boat scarcely a word was spoken ; the sky was gray ; the water of the canal was still as an oil-tank ; the tranquillity was only disturbed by an old man who was scooping water out of the canal with a long shovel and flinging it over the quay to lay the dust, regardless of the convenience of the passers-by, some of whom mildly protested. Soon after starting we met a barge with a large family on board, towed along by the eldest brother, the eldest sister, and an ugly bastard bull-dog, harnessed together, one in front of the other, the dog leading. Then we sighted a bridge, apparently only about six feet above the water ; we neared the bridge, but the bridge neither swung round nor rose in the air. How were we to pass under it? The situation became alarming the nearer we approached. Georges and Thérèse grew pale, but the *stoomboot* continued its course. Then, with a rattle of chains, the funnel was lowered, and to save our lives we tourists on the cabin roof lay flat on our stomachs, much to the amusement of the native passengers, who had prudently remained on the deck below. The passage of this first bridge taught us the way down the ladder, and explained the lowness of the benches.

Soon we sighted Schiedam, surrounded by a cordon of gigantic windmills, which give it the air of a fortified town crowned with towers. Thence we glided along rapidly through vast plains of pasture-land, full of black and white cattle and horses. On either side were broad, flowery meadows, traversed by long lines of poplars and willows. In the distance we saw village spires. Often the meadows were far below the level of the canal. The solitude was only enlivened by two or three chocolate-colored sails which loomed into view from time to time. The steamer would slacken speed to see what course they would take, and then they would glide past us, their sail-boom grazing our heads. Other boats would come along, with a man pushing against the bow with a long pole fixed at right angles; others again were hauled by trios of dogs, men, and women. At intervals all along the route were windmills, not the broken-down, piteous windmills of France, but triumphant monsters which even Don Quixote would have hesitated to attack. Some are built of masonry, round or octagon, like mediæval towers; other smaller mills are of wood, perched on the point of a pyramid of brickwork. Most of them are thatched and encircled half-way up by a wooden gallery. The windows are neatly draped with white curtains, the doors are painted green, and over the door is a sign indicating the nature of the mill. The small mills are mostly used for pumping water and draining the meadows; the larger ones are used for all sorts of purposes, grinding corn, limestone, or colza, tobacco manufacturing, paper making, and, above all, sawing. Most of the mills between Rotterdam and Delft are saw-mills. They are placed close at the water's edge, and surrounded by reservoirs in which are seen floating thousands of logs of wood, which the lumbermen manipulate with long hooks, but always silently. The only noise you hear is the monotonous tic-tac of the windmills. The villages along the canal are equally silent. The houses are built at the very edge of the water, and the women do their washing from their doorstep in the canal itself, while the watch-dog sleeps in his basket, and the big, square-headed, heavy Dutch cats lie basking in the sun.

From time to time the stern of the *stoomboot* was steered inshore, and a passenger got on or off, and so on we glided sleepily through brilliant green pastures and windmills, and beds of rushes, all calm and tranquil until we came to the village of Overschie. Here there was a tangle of boats coming in opposite directions; the canal was narrow, and everything seemed to be in an inextricable mess. The steamer slowed, not a word was said, and the men calmly went to work with poles and cleared the passage. Not a single impatient word was uttered, and yet the confusion was formidable. At the risk of seeming to repeat myself, I cannot help again remarking the curious silence and tranquillity of this trip. There was no exchange of greetings between the crews of the barges; the men on our boat did not talk; the cattle in the meadows did not low; there were no birds twittering and flying about, nothing winged visible but ducks and occasionally a seagull, and even the ducks were silent and cleared out of the way of the approaching steamer without uttering a single couac. Naturally we could not help being struck by this phenomenal calmness and stillness of the Dutch people and of Dutch landscape. Wherever we went afterwards, we made the same observation. The whole country seemed asleep, like the waters of the canals, and you travel as it were in a dream. The canal-boat is the real vehicle from which to see Holland, and you will get a truer and more complete impression of the country of dykes, polders, canals, and windmills, from an afternoon's journey on a *trekshuit* or a *stoomboot* than from days of travelling from town to town in a railway car.

Naturally, it strikes the traveller as exceedingly

odd to find that the level of the country is just as often as not below the level of the navigable canals, while the whole country itself is intersected by a dense net-work of minor canals, into which or out of which there are innumerable little wind-mills constantly pumping water. And over this country there circulates a cool, fresh, moist air, impregnated with that savory odor of peat which is characteristic of Holland. The Hollanders have no coal, and the wood that they possess has been raised painfully and planted with jealous care to consolidate the land conquered from marshes or from the sea. These trees are too precious to burn, and so the national fuel is fibrous earth, which gives a comfortable, homely smell to the towns and villages, suggestive of tea-brewing in brilliantly burnished utensils, and of cosy fires smouldering away in neatly brushed-up hearths. Every traveller will understand this matter of national odors; they tell one every-thing, the latitude, the distance from the pole or the equator, from the coal-mines or the aloes plant, the climate, the seasons, the habits, the history even of a country. Every land favored by nature has its aromatic perfumes and its odoriferous smoke that speaks to the imagination. The smell of the peat smoke of Holland brings up to the mind the whole existence and history of the country of dykes, polders, and canals.

It may be said of the three principal Dutch

towns, that at Rotterdam the Dutchman makes his fortune, at Amsterdam he consolidates it, and at the Hague he spends it. The Hague is one of the least Dutch of Dutch towns. It reminds one at once of Versailles, of the Parc Monceau at Paris, and of the West End of London. It has just enough local features to give it a peculiar charm, and just enough elegant cosmopolitism to render it a European capital. At the Hague we find a native aristocracy, a foreign aristocracy, and imposing wealth established in conditions of ample and somewhat haughty luxury. The Hague is even a royal city, and it only wants a palace worthy of its rank in order to make all the traits of its physiognomy in harmony with its final destiny. You feel that its old stathouders were princes; that these princes were in their way Medicis; that they had a taste for the throne; that they ought to have reigned somewhere, and that it was not their fault if it was not here.

Thus the Hague is an exceedingly distinguished town, as it has a right to be, for it is very rich, and riches entail as a duty fine manners and magnificence; it is correct and peaceable; its streets are broad and handsome; its houses substantial and brilliant with paint, varnish, and burnished brasses; the waters of its canals are green, and reflect only the bright verdure of their banks. The woods of the Hague are admirable. Born of the caprice of a prince, as its Dutch name, s'Gravenhaag—Count's Park — indicates, formerly a hunting-seat of the Counts of Holland, the Hague has a passion for trees, and the forest is the favorite promenade of the inhabitants, the place where they hold their fêtes, their concerts, their military parades, and their rendezvous. The great domestic luxury of the Hague is an abundance of plants and flowers. The gardens, the houses, the verandas, the windows, are full of rare plants ; on the lawns are noble animals grazing at liberty; for the Hague has inherited from the Nassau princes the taste for gardening, for forest promenades in sumptuous carriages, for menageries and other princely *fantaisies*. The architecture of the town reminds one of the French architecture of the seventeenth century. Its exotic luxury comes from Asia. Its practical comfort and solid homeliness reminds one so much of London that one can hardly say which town has served as a model for the other. In short, with its splendid promenades, its woods, its beautiful water-walks, its private mansions, its collections of pictures, its ancient palace where so much of the history of Holland has been made, the Hague is a town to be seen, and a town which predisposes to calm and studious meditation. The lake in the centre of the town, the Vidjer, is a most original spot. Imagine an immense reservoir surrounded by quays and palaces. To the right is a promenade planted with trees, and, beyond the trees,

7

mansions enclosed in their gardens; to the left is the Binnenhof, built in the thirteenth century, the residence of the stathouders, the scene of the massacre of Barneveldt. The palace walls are washed by the waters of the reservoir; its façade of red brick, its slate roofs, its morose air, its physiognomy of another age, its tragic souvenirs, give it that vague something which is peculiar to certain places famous in history. Beyond, in the distance, you see the cathedral spire; in the midst of the lake is a green island, where the swans preen themselves; above in the air and around the irregular roofs of the palace are swarms of swallows. All around perfect silence reigns, profound repose, complete oblivion of things present and past.

At the southern angle of the reservoir is the Mauritshuis, where the royal collection of pictures is now hung. What a contrast and what a lesson, as the painter Fromentin has remarked, are contained in these two neighboring palaces! The Binnenhof is full of the memories of William the Silent, of the brothers De Witt, of Barneveldt, of Maurice of Nassau, of Heinsius, of the States-General, which for fifty years held out against Spain and England, and dictated conditions to Louis XIV. In the Mauritshuis are the master-works of two painters, Rembrandt and Paul Potter. Every day some pilgrims from the four quarters of the world go and knock at the door of the museum; not half a dozen times in the year does a tourist disturb the solitude of the Binnenhof or the Buitenhof, or derange the spiders in their dust-spinning operations in the historic chamber of the States-General. Why should there be so much curiosity felt about a picture and so little about the historic palace where great statesmen and great citizens struggled most heroically for their country, their religion, and their liberty? The fact is that the heroes of history do not always owe their lasting renown to their own acts. A nation disappears with its laws, its manners, its conquests; there remains of its history but a fragment of marble or bronze, and this testimony is enough. By his intelligence, his courage, his political sense, and his public acts, Pericles was a very great man; but perhaps humanity would not know even his name if it were not embalmed in literature, and if he had not employed a friend of his, a great sculptor, to decorate the temples of Athens. Alcibiades was frivolous, dissipated, witty, foppish, libertine, though valiant when duty called him; and yet he is more universally spoken of than Solon, Plato, Socrates, or Themistocles. Was he wiser or braver than they? Did he serve better than they truth, justice, and the interests of his country? No. He simply had the advantage of an immense charm; he loved passionately all that was beautiful — women, books, statues, and pictures. Antony was an unfortunate general, a mediocre politician, a giddy ruler; but he had the good-fortune to love one of the most seductive women in history, that "rare Egyptian," as Shakespeare calls her, who was the incarnation of all beauty.

The ingenious James Howell, in one of his "Epistolæ Ho-Elianæ," remarks of the Dutch that their towns are beautiful and neatly built, but with such uniformity that who sees one sees all. The same observer remarks that the Hollander is slow, surly, and respectless of gentry and strangers, homely in his clothing, of very few words, and heavy in action. The Hollanders and their towns remain to-day very much the same as they were nearly three centuries ago when Howell wrote. The principal changes are that the national costume is no longer worn much except in the extreme north; that the national head-dresses of the different provinces are rapidly falling out of use; that there are railways all over the country and tramways all over the towns, even in such quiet places as Leyden and Utrecht, which the guide-books perversely describe as dead cities. Furthermore, Colman's starch, Huntley & Palmer's biscuits, Pears' soap, Singer's sewing-machines, Stephens's ink, English stationery, English cutlery, English children's books, and Bass's bitter pursue the traveller all over the Low Countries. Of Amsterdam I need say very little. Like Rotterdam, it is a city of quays and canals and brick façades, only it is more gloomy and dingy, and, as if the deepest red bricks were not dark enough, some of the Amsterdam houses are actually painted black. Built upon ninety islands, which are connected together by three hundred and fifty bridges, intersected by canals in every direction, Amsterdam is a sort of Northern Venice, a Venice enlarged and made ugly, and not particularly agreeable to explore in detail. But the first view of the town as you approach in the train is very striking, even after having seen Rotterdam. You seem to have before you a veritable forest of windmills rising in the forms of towers, spires, pyramids, and cones, and agitating their colossal wings high above the housetops. Amid these mills rise factory chimneys, spires of strange architecture, roofs, pinnacles, and points of unknown forms, masts of ships, and, beyond, other windmills fading away over the surrounding plains. The effect is grandiose and imposing. But for characteristic Dutchness, if I may so express myself, and quiet, sleepy charm, I prefer Leyden and Utrecht, which towns travellers are generally advised not to visit because they contain few monuments, museums, or "sights." To my mind one of the great charms of Holland is that, apart from the incomparable picture-galleries of Amsterdam, Haarlem, and the Hague, the country has no special sights; the chief pleasure of the traveller consists in taking in general impressions which are utterly new and strange, and he may visit almost any town in Holland without feeling himself in duty bound to examine any particular monument, church, or palace. Unlike their neighbors, the Belgians, the Hollanders are not great in architecture. In all their towns you feel that the people were in a hurry to install themselves on the mud they had conquered from sea or marsh, but, being concerned solely with their commerce, their labor, their individual and limited comfort, they never thought, even in their grandest days of prosperity of building palaces. Ten minutes passed on the Grand Canal at Venice, and ten others passed on the Kalverstraat at Amsterdam, will tell you all that history has to teach about the genius of the two countries. In the land of Spinosa and Rembrandt, the windows of the houses taking up more space than the walls, the little balconies with their flower-pots, the spy-mirrors fixed on the windows, the careful neatness of the blinds and curtains, indicate that in this climate the winter is long, the sun unfaithful, the light sparing of its rays, and life of necessity sedentary; that open-air revelries are rare, and indoor joys lively; and that the eye, the mind, and the soul naturally contract in these conditions that form of patient, attentive, minute investigation, as it were with a screwing up of the eyes, which is common to all Dutch thinkers, from the metaphysicians down to the painters.

At Leyden I stayed a whole week without seeing a single sight. The country all around is more wooded than any other part of Holland, and Leyden itself is a perfect paradise. The canals there are beautiful beyond expression, and the water almost limpid and quite unlike the black fluid we had seen at Amsterdam and Rotterdam; the people are better-looking, especially the women and children, who appeared to spend much time in basking in the sun and loafing in the beautiful public gardens of the city. The streets of Leyden are lined with fine shops brilliantly lighted up at night, and reflected in the tranquil waters of the canals. I may remark generally that the Dutch shops are all admirably illuminated and give a peculiar aspect to the streets at night, for this reason : the Dutch houses are narrow; the shop fronts, generally of plate glass, occupy the whole width of the ground floor; the upper part of the façade remains in gloom. The consequence is that when the shops are lighted up they form, as it were, one continuous band of light, which seems to support the houses. The dark upper stories represent old-fashioned Holland; the dazzling ground-floor represents the new life of fashion, luxury, and elegance. Thanks to this lavish burning of gas the Dutch towns are quite gay at night ; the streets are full of promenaders, and in fact the evening is the busy part of the day for the shopkeepers. But what delighted

me most at Leyden was the daylight aspect of
the town, with its canals bordered with fine old
trees and quaintly gabled houses, the innumerable bridges, the swans, the calm, the happy-look-
ing people, the carillon of the cathedral, the gardens and water-walks. One could not desire a
more delightful place for tranquil meditation, and
as a university town it is almost as perfect as
Oxford. But alas! the University of Leyden
has fallen from its high estate, and only a few
hundred students now tread the streets where
thousands used to crowd to hear Lipsius, Vossius,
Heinsius, Gronovius, Hemsterhuys, the great
Julius Cæsar Scaliger, and other mighty doctors
whose names are immortal in the annals of classical learning. Vanished, too, the house of those
famous printers, the Elzevirs. In 1807 the whole
quarter was destroyed by the explosion of a powder magazine, and with it the printing establishment of Jean Elzevir, "so renowned throughout
all Christendom for its fine type," as pompous old
Percival says in his quaint volume, "Les Délices
de la Hollande."

Our stay at Leyden was rendered all the more
agreeable by the excellent hospitality of the Hôtel
du Lion d'Or, which must have been a palace
in the old days of Leyden's prosperity. The
entrance hall is very lofty; the front door is a
massive and finely sculptured piece of eighteenth
century *rocaille* work; the floor is of white mar-

ble veined with rose, and the walls are wainscoted some way up with the same marble; at the end of the hall, opposite the dining-room door, is a delicately carved marble *fontaine* with a silver swan's-neck tap, where you may wash your fingers. The staircase, with its massive handrail of mahogany, is roofed over with an octagon lantern with small square pane windows, the lantern being decorated with *mascarons* and scrolls at the eight angles, while in the middle on the white ground is a dark blue dial with a gold finger and gold lettering. This dial is connected with the weathercock on the roof outside and indicates the direction of the wind. What could be more characteristic of an inclement Northern climate, what more suggestive of a Dutchman's love of comfort, than this interior weathercock indicator? The idea struck me as very sensible, and the mysterious and silent movement of the hand on the dial gave a pleasing animation to this stately staircase.

Quitting sleepy Leyden, with its souvenirs of ancient learning and ancient splendor, we made an excursion in an unpoetical steam tramway to Katwyk-an-Zee, a little sea-side village much frequented by the Dutch, and within three quarters of an hour's ride from Leyden. The journey is interesting. The steam tram rattles along through fields, between little canals, along village streets lined with trees cropped fan-shape, whose branches rustle against the windows. All these cottages are clean and excessively tidy, and each window is provided with that blue wire-gauze screen in a black frame which is one of the distinguishing features of window furniture throughout Holland. You pass the *Château* of Endegeest, where Descartes wrote his principal philosophical and mathematical works; about half-way you come to a seminary of priests, whom you see clad like the characters in the pictures of the seventeenth century, smoking their cigars and pipes calmly in a garden gay with all kinds of flowers. Then gradually the country becomes less smiling, and you sight a belt of low, irregular gray hillocks or sand dunes. The land grows more desolate and sandy, the rich green grass of the Dutch pastures yields place to wiry sand-squitch, and you see only here and there a sunken patch of potatoes or black oats growing some four or five feet below the level of the sand. Then deep down amid the dunes, in a sort of ravine, there is a pond of black water, and in the pond a green barge. This is the Leyden Canal boat, and here is the termination of the Leyden Canal, with which the Rhine has consented to amalgamate. What a piteous ending for the glorious stream that tumbles tumultuously over the rocks of Schaffhausen, passes triumphantly past Ehrenbreitstein, and reflects in its long course princely castles, Gothic cathedrals, historical ruins, famous vineyards, and storied mountains! Can that poor little dingy stream flowing mildly between two flat and desolate banks be the Rhine that we have all heard celebrated in music and song?

Proceeding a little farther on at a higher level we come to the village of Katwyk, whose streets are beautifully paved with red and yellow bricks, and lined with fishermen's cottages with gardens hedged around with many-colored fragments of broken-up old boats. On this queer fencing the small nets are hung to dry, while the long nets used for herring-fishing may be seen darkening the slopes of the dunes with their black meshes. At the end of the village you find yourself on the summit of an immense dyke which runs away along the coast in either direction, and in front of you stretches the North Sea, gray, wrinkled, rough, and desolate. At a short distance along the dyke you come to a black channel running into the sea at right angles, and banked in on either side by huge slabs of black granite, bordered with an edging of stakes and fascines to break up the waves. At the head of this canal, on a line with the dykes, whose continuity is uninterrupted at this spot, are four huge pillars of gray stone surmounted by a tremendous blank wall, built of Cyclopean blocks of stone. Between the pillars are five sets of sluice gates. It is thanks to these sluice gates that the poor old Rhine finally gets into the sea. Formerly it lost itself utterly in the swamps of Holland, and presented the strange phenomenon of a river without a mouth. Under the reign of Louis Bonaparte, in 1807, the waters of the Rhine were collected in a canal and conducted to the sea by a series of locks and sluice gates which form the most grandiose monument in Holland and the most admirable piece of hydraulic engineering in Europe. The locks of Katwyk are three in number. The first has two pairs of sluice gates, the second four pairs, and the third nearest the sea five pairs. When the tide runs in the gates are closed to prevent the sea-water running into the lock, for the tide rises four mètres high up the gates and is often far above the level of the canal, and consequently of all the country protected by the dykes. When the tide runs out the gates are opened for five or six hours, and the water stored up in the three locks is let out at the rate of 3000 cubic mètres a second. The dykes themselves look like more or less regular earthworks of sand planted in diagonal lines with tufts of squitch grass.

A more desolate, cold, dreary, inhospitable spot than Katwyk after sunset, or in the gray of the evening, I never saw. The wild and tumultuous dunes that slope down inland beyond the dykes like monstrous petrified waves, the monotonous desolation of the sand-covered dykes, the roaring of the horrid sea, and that still, black channel running up to the blankest and dismallest of walls against which, at high water, the waves dash and storm in vain—all this is profoundly desolate and profoundly impressive. Here, indeed, the Hollanders, in their calm and morose way, say to the sea, "Thus far shalt thou come and no farther!" And the North Sea has to confess itself conquered and leave the Hollanders to cultivate their tulips in peace, and to churn their butter in prosperity behind the enormous and wonderful fortress of the dykes and locks of Katwyk.

A TRIP TO NAPLES.

When the Continental railway companies decide to reform their rolling-stock and to make up their trains in the American fashion, with restaurant, smoking-room, rocking-chairs, bookstall, and other conveniences all on board, Europe will have made a great step towards deserving that reputation of civilization on which she already prides herself. Alas! when one sees the accommodation which the railway companies place at the disposal of ordinary mortals for a fifteen hours' journey, one is forcibly reminded that European civilization in matters relating to travelling is only very relative and certainly nothing to boast about. Nevertheless, in spite of the discomfort, I always enjoy the first long jaunt at the beginning of the summer holidays. It is pleasing to think that you are realizing a long-cherished project, that for a time you are going to live a new life in new scenes, to see new faces and new costumes, and even to make the acquaintance of new cookery. For my part, too, I think there is no more agreeable distraction than that of gazing out of the window at the moving panorama of plain, river, and mountain which unrolls itself as the train rushes past and leaves on the memory a rapid but none the less striking impression. On the day when I left Paris a night's rain had laid the dust, the air was fresh, and the heavens were charged with scudding clouds which played hide-and-seek with the sun, and produced all day most varying and curious skies. It was neither too hot nor too cold, too cloudy nor too sunny; and in these conditions it was charming to contemplate the rich vegetation of Burgundy, the vast plains where the hay-wagons were being drawn by cream-white or fulvous oxen marching solemnly with stately tread, the Seine winding its way past pleasant villages and gray old towns, and the vines climbing up the slopes. The Anglo-Saxon gentlemen in our carriage persisted in mistaking the vines for "dwarf hops." I did not enlighten them, not wishing to give myself any air of superior knowledge.

"Tonnerre, vingt cinq minutes d'arrêt, buffet!" cried the porters as the train slowed along the platform, and we all skipped out of the carriages and made haste to reach the refreshment-room, where steaming soup was awaiting us in forty and odd plates. A well-drilled squadron could not have fallen into eating position with more precision and rapidity than our train-load. Not a second was lost; there was no crush or crowd;

and suddenly every seat was occupied, and the
silence was brusquely broken by the simultaneous
clanking of forty and odd soup-spoons against
forty and odd soup-plates. The meal was very
good, and served with such rapidity and good
order that in less than twenty minutes each of
us had taken soup, fish, and roast, a vegetable,
fowl and salad, sweets, cheese, and coffee! And
yet, in spite of my gastronomic preoccupations, I
had time to observe the lady who presided over
this buffet, a tall, stately, white-skinned, black-
haired Burgundian, with the walk and bearing of
a goddess, and a predisposition to obesity; but
still, I should say, as fine a woman as the Venus
of Milo, and indisputably far more complete.

Leaving Tonnerre, we traversed the rich vineyards of the Côte d'Or, passing from time to time
some quaint old village perched on a hill, with
its church spire rising above the trees, and its
house-roofs and walls running over the whole
gamut of reds, browns, and grays, and mingling
in soft harmony with the various greens of the
luxuriant vegetation. Passing Dijon, we arrived in
a region of mountains, covered with gloomy, dark-
foliaged trees; then we sighted the Saône river,
which kept us company down to Lyons. At Lyons
I stayed a few hours, and drove round the town.
The park at Lyons, with its lake, its palm-houses,
its immense aviary, trailed over with roses, its
deer paddock, and its enormous beds of rose-trees

planted in profusion all over the lawns, is as beautiful a public garden as I have ever seen. Lyons itself, with its lofty houses climbing up the precipitous heights of La Croix Rousse, where are the principal silk manufactories, is picturesque enough taken as a whole, but neither its streets nor its monuments will excite the admiration of the traveller. After dinner I had the good-fortune to find some mountebanks on the Place Perrache, and spent some time at a "Concert Tunisien," where three girls and an Arab formed the company, the star of which was Mdlle. Fatma, who had had "the advantage of posing for several celebrated painters, and of having her portrait exhibited in the Salon, when the critics of Paris found her form perfect in grace and elegance." So said the showman, whereupon Mdlle. Fatma sent round the hat for her *petits bénéfices*, and, clad in cloth of gold and carmine silk, proceeded to execute the sword dance, while the Arab thumped an earthenware drum, the other two girls shook tambourines, and the showman strummed a monotonous air on a wheezy piano. The effect was suave and digestive.

From Lyons to Orange my journey was continued in the dark. At Orange I woke up and found myself in a country of meadows and orchards and plantations of mulberry-trees dimly visible between the pale moonlight and the golden glow which was already illumining the eastern

8

sky. I was in Provence, in the country of Mistral and Daudet, in the country of the troubadours and the cigalas. Happily, the sky was cloudless; at last I had escaped from the region of rain and gloom. Avignon, Tarascon, Arles, Miramas, follow in quick succession, and the country becomes more and more curious. Vast fertile plains alternate with rocky wastes and marshes, and in the distance you see Mont Ventoux and the chains of the Alpilles, with their strangely jagged outlines standing out in deep violet relief against the clear sky. Then you pass by a series of blue lakes smiling in the midst of a wilderness of yellow and brown rocks, and so to Marseilles.

To my mind Marseilles is one of the most delightful towns in Europe during a stay of two or three days. The Cannebière with its cafés and the incessant and varied movement of the street; the animation of the port; the afternoon concerts under the trees in the Allée de Meillan; the splendid promenades; the vibrating accent of the natives; the mixture of African and Levantine elements in the crowd: all this affords endless material for restful musing. My intention in coming to Marseilles was to spend some time in eating the native dish *bouillabaisse* in perfection and then to proceed by sea to Naples. The first part of my programme was executed faithfully, and repeatedly my steps carried me along the Corniche Road towards the restaurant of La

Réserve, where the dynasty of Roubion dispenses most excellent and rare dishes on shady terraces almost literally overhanging the Mediterranean. Several times I partook of that especially local dish *bouillabaisse*, and always with new pleasure; for the sauce, with its golden - brown *croustades*, is one of the most savory stews ever made—a *coulis* of the "trimmings" of a hundred little fishes freshly caught and distilled slowly over a smokeless fire, with fennel, bay-leaves, saffron, Manilla pepper, salt, onions, a tomato, and, above all, the unctuous oursin, a sort of sea - urchin, which abounds on the rocks of the Mediterranean. Even a little garlic may be added to this liquid treasure, which is only the preface of the great poem of stewed fish composed of the perfumed rascasse, the red mullet, the whiting, the pagel, the orade, the loup, the galinette, and other fishes of the Southern waters, as the Marseillais poet Méry says:

> " Et d'autres oubliés par les icthyologues,
>   Fins poissons que Neptune, aux feux d'un ciel ardent,
>   Choisit à la fourchette et jamais au trident."

While rendering due homage to *bouillabaisse*, I did not forget two excellent and little - known wines—Nerthe and Tavel. The latter, grown at Avignon on the slopes opposite to where Château-neuf des Papes used to grow, is a luscious drink, combining the bouquet of Spanish wines with the piquancy and lightness of the wines of France. I recommend it to amateurs.

After a few days' gastronomic and other explorations in Marseilles, I embarked on a fine steamer bound for Shanghai, and a run of thirty-six hours brought us into the Bay of Naples. Vesuvius was panting forth red flashes in the distance, and the promenades and streets of the city, all illuminated on the occasion of some fête or other, formed as it were an immense crown of luminous pearls. No sooner had we arrived in the port than small boats began to crowd around the ship, several of them having on board musicians, who bade us a harmonious welcome to Naples. Alas, the Prefect of Naples was not so ready to receive us! On the contrary, he had just heard that very evening of the outbreak of cholera at Toulon, and, in accordance with orders from the government at Rome, he regretted to be obliged to put us in quarantine. So the yellow flag was hoisted, and early next morning we passengers for Naples were deposited in the lazzaretto on the island of Nissida. The surprise was as complete as it was disagreeable, and there was but little consolation to be derived from the reflection that it did not fall to the lot of many summer tourists to be imprisoned in a plague-house.

Our arrival at the lazzaretto caused great excitement among the guardians of the establishment, who insisted on keeping us at a respectful distance, and by their gestures and bearing convinced us that it is by no means agreeable to be suspected of being the harbingers of the pest. Nevertheless, as we all felt healthy and well, we did our best to keep up our spirits and to make ourselves as comfortable as possible. The island of Nissida is delightfully situated in the gulf of Pozzuoli, just opposite the southwest spur of the Posilippo. It appears to be an extinct crater, opening towards the south and forming a little bay, around two thirds of which is built the lazzaretto, while the other part is occupied by a mole, a lighthouse, and barracks, behind which rises a hill covered with olive-trees and crowned by a vast circular building used as a convict prison. The old lazzaretto, in which we were imprisoned, is a picturesque old place built in the Moorish style, with arcades and flat roofs—a series of queer blocks perched on the rocks and communicating with each other by a most complicated system of staircases, inclined planes, and passages, interrupted by massive doors and iron gates. A causeway of black stone connects the old lazzaretto with the new one and with the neighboring island on which the prison is situated. The chambers where we were lodged were lofty, whitewashed rooms, with glazed tile floors imitating mosaic, furnished with a few rush-seated chairs, a little table, a wash-bowl on an iron stand, three or four pairs of iron trestles supporting boards on which are laid the quarantine mattresses —simple canvas bags filled with dried maize husks. Our attendants were fishermen, who volunteered their services, and ran the risk of catching all sorts of diseases for the consideration of fifty cents a day and whatever gratuities the victims of quarantine chose to give them. The food, supplied by the restaurant of the lazzaretto and served in the chambers, was good, but very dear for the country — $2 a day for two meals and coffee in the morning.

The rooms, it is true, were of monastic simplicity, and the whole place smelt overpoweringly of phenol, but each room had a casement window opening on balconies overhanging the sea and commanding a delicious view. On one side you see Pozzuoli; a picturesque rock covered with white and red houses, and in the background a line of hills which in the course of the day passes through the most varied shades of gray and blue and rose. On the other side, you look across the extreme breadth of the gulf of Naples as far as Sorrento and Capri. If one were only free it would be delightful to wander about this island, to admire the panorama of the surrounding scenery, and to marvel at the blueness of the Mediterranean, which washes its shores, and displays, through the pellucid mirror of its waters, its bed covered with myriads of sea-plants which glisten in the brilliant sunlight like silvery flowers. So strong is the light and so clear the water that from the height of our balcony, a hundred feet above the water, we could see the bottom of the bay with its carpet of anemones and weeds.

Still, in spite of our captivity, we were not absolutely wretched. The band to which I belonged comprised some twenty people, including a Sicilian who was an excellent conjuror and a fair guitariste; three Milanese ladies who sang like nightingales; a retired French gendarme who passed his time in dangling his feet in the sea with a view to dissolving his corns, and in furbishing his threadbare frockcoat with an old tooth-brush; a Parisian familiar with the repertory of the cafés-concerts; a ballerina from the San Carlo theatre who had been fulfilling an engagement in Paris, and whom I had frequently applauded at the Eden Théâtre from a stall in the front row—an excellent introduction, as you may well imagine—the mother of the ballerina, and half a score ragged Italian peasant people who adapted themselves to our society with that easy but never disagreeable familiarity which characterizes the Latins.

Before we had been on the island an hour we were all good friends; and, after a little excusable lamentation, we determined to make the best of our lot and to open communications with the mainland. In these negotiations the ballerina was most successful, and through her friends in Naples we were supplied with playing-cards, guitars, castagnettes, tobacco, and edible delicacies. Thanks to dancing, singing, and smoking, we passed the time almost gayly; we organized all kinds of games; we were allowed during exercise hours to jump off the quay and swim about the bay within certain limits and under the eye of sentries armed with guns; we were even allowed to dive for sea-urchins, but for this a special permission had to be obtained, because the sentries did not like to lose sight of us, even for a few seconds. Of these amusements, of the splendid sunlight, of the heat always tempered by the sea air, of the thrumming of the guitars, of the whirling wildness of the tarantella, of the soft Italian songs that floated through the air at nightfall, of the distant cries of the fishermen crossing the bay, of this whole week of pure animal life, I have a souvenir that will be readily comprehended by those who have had the misfortune, or perhaps we should say the privilege, to be isolated for a time from ordinary life, to be deprived of all possibility of initiative, and reduced to the necessity of merely living on one's own resources and on those of chance companions. The feeling of irritation soon disappears, especially in favorable conditions of climate; one becomes resigned to one's fate; and, as long as deep ennui can be avoided, the mere vegetative or lizard-like existence offers certain positive joys. Nevertheless, in spite of our gay philosophy and our indefatigable guitars, we could not forget that we were prisoners. We could not help regarding ourselves, and especially each batch of new-comers, with distrust, fearing every moment that cholera might break out among us. The lazzaretto, too, soon began to fill up. Every day three or four ships deposited a score or two of passengers, who were stowed away in separate buildings under special guardians. Finally, on the day we were liberated, some 500 men, women, and children were crowded together like cattle on this little island, and our suspense had become more and more trying, for, until the eve of our liberation, we did not know whether we were to be imprisoned for ten, twenty, or thirty days.

I need not say how great was our delight and how boisterous our manifestations of joy when we took leave of the director of the lazzaretto, and set foot on the mainland at the little village of Coroglio, where carriages were in waiting to convey us to Naples, and where I was taken charge of by the most amiable and vivacious of Neapolitan hostesses, who had brought her whole family to welcome the long-expected prisoner.

What a delightful drive it was through a most beautiful and fertile stretch of country, rich in vines, olives, fig-trees, and maize fields! And how curious the suave contessina was to know

how I had fared in that dreadful lazzaretto! And
how glad I was to reach her house on the Riviera
di Chiaja, and how confused by the rattling of the
carriage over the pavement, by the swarming, picturesque crowd of men and animals, and by the
deafening din of chattering and shouting that
filled the streets! After the calm of Nissida the
animation of Naples on this sunny July morning
was simply bewildering.

"But what a strange idea," I hear the reader
exclaim—"what a strange idea to go to Naples in
July! The heat must be terrible!" On the contrary, the heat is delicious, because it is always tempered by the sea-breeze, and never stuffy and op-
pressive like the heat of London or of Paris. The
room where I was lodged, in a house on the Chiaja,
within a stone's-throw of the sea, was as cool and
airy as one could wish, and, through an opening
in the light-green Venetian shutters, I had a match-
less view over the glistening waters of the bay;
to the left, the slope of Vesuvius dotted with
the white and rose and blue cottages of Castellamare and Sorrento; to the right, the heights of
Posilippo covered with villas and verdure of rich,
fresh green; in front, the blue sea and the island
of Capri; overhead, a sky of the purest and most
luminous blueness. The Riviera itself is the
Champs Elysées of Naples—a series of gardens and
avenues and promenades running along the seashore; the Rotten Row of the city, where, between

six and eight in the evening, all the Neapolitan
swells come to see and to be seen, in more or less
elegant equipages, and with a grand display of
coachmen and footmen in livery. What more
could one desire? The first ten days that I
passed at Naples were charming. In the morning we used to take a boat, pull out into the bay,
and bathe. A stroll in the public gardens carried us on to breakfast. Our hostess, a lover of
music, seemed always to have a selection of
maestri at her feet, and the afternoon passed
rapidly until it was time to change our coats for
the promenade. When the sun began to sink
the contessina's landau arrived at the door; the
horses were lanky-looking beasts, but full of life,
and brilliantly harnessed with a profusion of gilt
trappings; the coachman, with his gray tweed
livery and gray hat with a blue cockade, had the
stiffness and angularity of his Anglo-Saxon col-
leagues; the reins and whip were decorated with
gay wool *pompons;* and the whole turn-out had a
dash of color and gaudiness which seemed thoroughly in harmony with the Southern climate
where we were, and where a rose-colored house
with ultramarine window-shades does not shock
the eye, so intense is the light and so great its
harmonizing influence. After the promenade
came dinner and more music and more *maestri*,
with beautifully combed hair, glossy moustaches,
and immense black eyes, and then we would sit

on the balcony in the moonlight, and need no
shawls or wrappers, as in Northern summer resorts
with their treacherous and chilly evenings. To
my mind, Naples in July is perfectly agreeable as
far as climate is concerned.

However, it is not my object to defend Naples.
I found it agreeable, and, above all, I found the
Neapolitan *cuisine*, as served at the contessina's
table, very delicate and erudite. Great dishes here
are fresh anchovies, *alice*, which you hear cried all
over the town ; little fat oysters, which cost sixpence a dozen ; cucumber flowers, culled when
the fruit is just forming, and fried in oil, with a
sprinkling of flour ; gourds cut into chips and
fried in the same way ; and, above all, a shell-fish
soup which I recommend to gourmets. The
preface of this gastronomic poem is a *coulis* of
smooth-leaved parsley fried in oil, or in butter if
you dislike oil ; to this basis you add tomatoes,
already well-boiled and drained : this mixture is
gently boiled, and hot water added to produce the
necessary quantity of bouillon. Then the shell-
fish—which have in the meantime been opened
by being thrown into hot water—are added to the
boiling bouillon, and the whole allowed to simmer
gently. The soup thus decocted is poured into a
tureen, garnished with *croustades* of white bread
fried golden brown in oil or butter, and so served
hot and savory. The shell-fish used here are
small cockles and other flat *coquillages* of similar

kind. The parsley is not chopped fine—the leaves are simply divided and float temptingly in the bouillon; the only seasoning required is pepper.

While I am still on the subject of the table I must reveal the secret of a salad which our amiable hostess prepared for us with her own white hands. Take sufficient of sweet pimentoes cut into thick slices, of tomatoes sliced similarly, of black olives, and of capers; season with salt and pepper; add slices of preserved anchovies, oil, and wine vinegar; turn the whole diligently; eat, digest, and be happy. This invigorating and refreshing salad is most appropriately named *rinforza*.

Leaving out of the question the luxurious existence of the local aristocracy and of the cosmopolitan population of visitors, the civilization of Naples may be said to have remained stationary since the Middle Ages. The old town is a network of narrow streets scarcely wider than those of Pompeii, and running up and down the three hills of Saint Elmo, Capo di Monte, and Pizzafalcone. Many of these streets are interrupted by flights of steps, and available only for foot or donkey traffic; others wind about under arches and vaults; and all are lined with lofty houses of gray, white, rose, or yellow color, with green Venetian shutters and balconies. The ground floor is invariably occupied by little shops, and the upper rooms are dwellings. A more busy, varied, and amusing scene than one of these narrow streets cannot be imagined. At the corner you invariably find a water-seller, installed at a little counter decorated with shining brass ornaments and provided with piles of lemons, half a dozen bottles of anisette, absinthe, and other liquors, stone demi-johns containing ferruginous, sulphurous, and other waters, and, at each end, two slender barrels swinging on pivots and containing fresh water kept deliciously cool by a casing of snow brought from the neighboring mountains. The *aqua fresca* sold at these innumerable street-stalls is delicious, and, with the addition of two or three drops of anisette, forms the favorite drink of the Neapolitans. Entering the street, we find a most motley crowd of hawkers of all kinds, some carrying their wares on their heads, and others accompanied by donkeys or mules laden with tomatoes, green figs, plums, and other fruits and vegetables, shaded by waving green branches. The street-hawker is so deeply rooted an institution at Naples that he has been able to ruin a company which went to great expense to provide the city with elegant iron markets like those of Paris. These markets, situated in various quarters of the town, failed utterly, and are now employed for riding-schools and other uses. The Neapolitan house-wife insists on being served at her door, or rather at her window, from which she lowers a basket attached to a rope, and bargains furiously over two sous' worth of plums. This constant lowering of baskets from balconies shaded by flaming ultramarine blinds and draped with the family washing hung out to dry adds greatly to the amusing aspect of the streets. Then, in the morning and afternoon, the streets are encumbered by herds of goats and cows, led two by two with ropes. Both cows and goats have bells at their necks, and are milked in the presence of the consumer. The goats even walk up the staircases of the houses, and deliver their milk literally at the door, whether it be on the second floor or on the fifth. Where the streets are broad enough, they are crowded with carts of the most primitive construction, drawn by queer combinations of mules and donkeys and bullocks, often three abreast and one of each kind. The animal between the shafts has always a saddle rising high in the air and surmounted by a profusion of brass ornaments, including two or three weathercocks, which spin round as he advances, and which in their turn are surmounted by a horn, or a brass hand with the index and little finger extended so as to form the horns which are supposed to avert the *jettatura*, or evil eye. No man, woman, or child in Naples is without a talisman of some kind; the housefronts are covered with horns of all kinds, and often you will see hung over doors and windows an inflated black glove, with the index and little finger extended in the required position. At Naples superstition still retains strong hold, and, besides the horns to avert the evil eye, every dwelling is provided with an image of the Madonna, before which a lamp is kept burning night and day; and all along the streets you will see images and pictures of saints in niches, with little lamps burning before them. In the room where I was living there were, besides the Madonna with her lamp, three other images of saints: namely, Saint Gennaro, Saint Antonino, and Saint Joseph, to say nothing of a gorgeous company of dressed dolls representing the Nativity; while on the landing was an oil-painting of the Crucifixion, before which a lamp was kept burning at the expense of the tenants of the flat.

It is hopeless to attempt to convey in words an idea of the animation of these little streets. Besides the curious crowd of shouting hawkers and chattering passengers, and vehicles and cattle, there are swarms of children, who in these warm summer days are often allowed to run about stark naked.   And beautiful little creatures many of them are, with their bronzed skins, their regular features, and their large, soft eyes! Then, again, everybody lives in the street. The little shops are so entirely taken up by the broad family beds that there is no room left to move about, and the merchandise is displayed in the street. The shoemaker works in the street, surrounded by his women-kind; the tailor sits cross-legged on the footpath; the housewife peels her potatoes on the footpath. At night the gossiping and card-playing and eating and drinking all go on in the street. The whole life of the town is out of doors; but it is neither indolent nor squalid. On the contrary, each of the little shops is the scene of indefatigable and cheerful industry; and both the men and the women wear clean linen. The modern Neapolitan, far from being indolent and squalid, seems to me rather to merit the titles of frugal and industrious. Why, then, it may be asked, does he remain poor? Because the civilization of the city has not progressed with the age. At Naples the trades are carefully separated and, to a great extent, confined to certain quarters. One quarter of the town is inhabited almost exclusively by coppersmiths, another by wheelwrights, another by cabinet-makers, another by shoemakers, and so forth. As a final trait of the simplicity of manners and customs, I will mention a curious scene which I witnessed one afternoon. At the end of a small square surrounded by lofty and irregular house-fronts were ranged four long benches forming a square. Some fifty men and women were seated on these benches, and in the middle a bronzed, black-haired man, with a long black moustache and lantern jaws, was reading aloud, out of a thin, double-column folio, an Italian translation of "The

9

Three Musketeers." This man's trade, I was
told, is to read aloud, and he receives two cen-
times, or less than half a cent, from each person
who sits on his benches, and nothing from the
outside listeners who remain standing. I can
assure you Alexandre Dumas never had a better
reader or a more attentive audience.

The resistance of the people to exterior influences, the preservation of native habits, the customs, the conditions of existence, and even the
humor of the inhabitants—such are the phenomena that seem to me most curious and attractive to
the wanderer in foreign lands. Nowhere has the
national character persisted as it has at Naples.
In spite of the cosmopolitan stamp which the
presence of tourists has impressed on certain
quarters of the town, the main portion has escaped
entirely all foreign contact. In the narrow streets
of old Naples the people retain the ancient gestures, the ancient habits, the ancient language;
they are a ragged, laughing, singing people, whose
sole object in life is to enjoy life. The gayety of
Naples is perhaps its most striking characteristic;
it is a spontaneous, instinctive gayety like that of
young animals; in Naples you never see that expression of fatigue, gloom, sadness, and despair
which you remark on the faces of the lower classes
in Paris or other Northern towns; the Neapolitans
are vivacious, careless and expansive; they seem
happy to dwell in the finest spot on earth, and

they express their joy by an intensity of movement and noise and an exuberance of gestures
quite unparalleled. The very houses seem to be
animated and swarming with teeming life. In no
other city in Europe do you obtain this idea of
mere abounding life which the streets and quays
of Naples offer. There is life at every step;
from the house-tops to the door-step you find
noisy manifestations of vivacious humanity; the
streets and the quays literally ferment with busy
life; even the vast expanse of the bay is thickly
dotted with humanity afloat, chattering, singing,
thrumming guitars, joking, finding amusement in
the mere act of living, moving, and making a noise.

Naples has hardly any monuments. The various mighty nations who have successively occupied the city—Greeks, Oscans, Romans, Goths,
Byzantines, Normans, Germans, and Spaniards—
have left no palaces or castles or churches that
attract the visitor's eye. The street architecture
has no particular character. The general aspect
of the city is without splendor. The main charm
of the place is its unique situation and its splendid bay. The visitor to Naples, therefore, naturally spends most of his time in making excursions
around the bay. In whatever direction he goes he
will find a lavish display of the gifts of nature
which amply compensates for the paltriness of the
works of man. All around Naples the scenery
of mountain, valley, and plain is magnificent, and

the fertility is incredible.   You can hardly understand how, in this country, where in the summer
rain does not fall for months together, the verdure can remain so luxuriant and so fresh, whereas
in the comparatively damp and Northern climates
of France and England the verdure loses all its
freshness before midsummer.   The explanation
is the lightness of the volcanic soil, which permits
the vines, for instance, to strike their roots as
much as forty feet into the earth.   One never
tires of admiring the orange and the lemon trees
weighed down with their golden fruit, the fig-
trees black with figs, the groves of olives, of
pomegranates, of mulberries, and of all kinds of
fruit-trees, bearing with an abundance which we
rarely see in the North.   Here, too, the vines
grow as Virgil describes them, hanging in festoons
from tree to tree.   The whole country around
the Bay of Naples is a truly patriarchal land, rich
in wine and oil, a land of peaceful happiness,
with overhead a cloudless sky, and before you the
vast blue gulf dotted with beautiful islands.

Naples itself, I must confess, is not wholly a
paradise.   The port and the parts around the
port are dirty and foul-smelling, and the part of
the bay between Naples and Torre del Greco is
a dirty and dusty manufacturing quarter, occupied
by iron-works, tanneries, and macaroni manufactories.   It is by traversing this horrible suburb
that you begin one of the most charming excur-

sions that can be made—a moonlight drive half
round the Bay of Naples. The first ten miles
of the journey is a delusion and a snare. You
imagine that you are going to be driven along
the seashore, and instead you go jolting through
dirty suburbs, with macaroni hung out to dry on
bamboo canes on each side of the road. As you
approach Torre Annunziata the houses become
less and less substantial, the people look less happy, and on all sides you see a profusion of images
of the Madonna, with lamps burning before them,
in niches. All the walls are covered with crosses
drawn in whitewash. We are here on the territory of Vesuvius, the terrible burning mountain
which we see blazing intermittently at no great
distance, and which has time after time inundated
with burning lava the ground over which we are
travelling. In the moonlight we can distinguish
the various lava streams that have rolled down
the mountain and remain still in rugged and
strangely contorted sooty wastes, like a raging
mountain torrent petrified in its tumultuous mo-
tion.

At Castellamare, where Pliny, the naturalist,
perished while observing an eruption of Vesuvius,
the scenery begins to be ideal. Henceforward,
until we reach Sorrento, no words can describe
the calm beauty of the spectacle presented to the
eye. The road winds along the base of the
mountains which form the amphitheatre of the

bay and which rise up rugged and precipitous on one side of the road, while on the other side are gardens and orange groves sloping gently down to the sea. All along this road, for some fifteen miles, you enjoy a constant view of the immense Bay of Naples, 35 miles broad. You see its northwest point, Cape Misenum; the islands of Procida and Ischia; the heights of Pozzuoli; Naples, with its crown of lights; Vesuvius, with its red cockade of fire; and, southward, the beautiful island of Capri. Whether you contemplate the panorama by sunlight or by moonlight it seems so beautiful, so poetical, so ideal that you can hardly believe that it is real and not some magnificent piece of theatrical scenery.

All the little towns and villages along the road are delicious places, nestling in thick groves of oranges, lemons, pomegranates, vines, and olives, ideally peaceful spots which in the old Roman times were the favorite retreats of Augustus, Agrippa, Antoninus Pius, and other great and noble persons, and which are now the resort of the *élite* of the leisured classes of all nationalities. Sorrento, in particular, is largely occupied by the English, insomuch that most of the shops bear inscriptions in the English language.

From Sorrento you go by a little steamer in an hour and a half to Capri, where Tiberius built twelve villas and spent the last years of his life. Earthquakes have considerably changed the form

of the island since the Roman times. The palaces have been thrown down and buried, and very
little remains to be seen in the way of monuments
or curiosities. Modern Capri is a favorite winter
resort for the delicate, and one of the last refuges
of the artists of Italy, who have been successively
driven away from Florence and Rome by the increase in the cost of living due to the presence
of the court. Capri is a beautiful and sleepy
earthly paradise, a fertile hill, rising out of the
sea, and covered with fruit-trees and flowers and
little stony paths that lead to cosy villas. The
climate is perfect. Unlike many pleasant places in
Italy, Capri is absolutely free from malaria. The
natural charms of the island, its singular health-
fulness, and its out-of-the-world position have
attracted to it, besides the annual immigration of
winter visitors, a most curious cosmopolitan colony
of permanent residents—Englishmen, Americans,
Russians, and Germans — who have seen much
of the world, men who have been in wars and
duels, retired Don Juans, philosophers who have
come to the conclusion that the blue sky and the
light of the sun are the two things most essential
to happiness. Several of these waifs of civilization have married, either regularly or irregularly,
native Capriote women, who are famous for their
beauty and for the grace of their forms and movements. In short, there is a collection of queer
Anglo-Saxon characters on the island of Capri

which deserves to be carefully studied. At Capri there are very few men. The population consists mainly of women and girls, for many of the men have emigrated to South America, and others are absent for two or three years at a time coral fishing on the African coast. The consequence is that all the work of the island is done by women and girls. The garden and field work, the household work, and all the carrying is done by girls. One of the curious and beautiful sights of Capri is a procession of ten or a dozen native girls, dressed in gay-colored robes, walking up and down the hilly paths with the step of goddesses, each balancing a burden on her head, a pail of water, a small barrel of wine, or a block of stone. All the material for house-building, the mortar, the stones, the wood, is carried into position by girls. You see them climbing a ladder, with a pail of mortar on their heads, with a gracefulness and dignity of movement which reminds you of the bas-reliefs of the Parthenon or of the groups depicted on Greek vases.

In spite of the guide-books, I say go and see this country in the summer rather than in the winter. Do your carriage travelling in early morning and by moonlight, and vary it by sailing-boats and steamers. The stories about the great heat which is supposed to rage here in summer are full of exaggeration, and contain no more truth than the stories about the squalidity of the

Neapolitans or the multiplicity and importunity of the native beggars. My summer trip to the Bay of Naples remains the most delightful excursion I have ever made—so delightful, indeed, that I am not quite sure that I was not dreaming.

"Travelling," said Madame de Staël, is one of the saddest pleasures in life. Crossing unknown countries, hearing people speak a language which you scarcely understand, and seeing human faces without any relation with your past or with your future, means solitude without repose and isolation without dignity. This zeal and this haste to arrive at a place where nobody expects you, this agitation of which the only cause is curiosity, inspire us with but little esteem for ourselves." I thought of this remark of the turbaned blue-stocking as I sped, one morning, through the entrails of Mont Cenis, eager to reach Northern Italy, and to see all those marvels of painting, of sculpture, and of architecture which thousands had seen before me and thousands would see after me—those masterpieces of art which are more enduring than thrones and kingdoms, and whose glory is so great that words cannot describe it. And it was precisely this greatness of the glory of the masterpieces of art which seemed to me to excuse the eagerness which I felt to see them; for to see them is to do homage, and he that does homage nobly and to noble idols is edified and augments his happiness. Madame de Staël was afflicted with excess of personality, and this is the reason why she spoke evil of foreign travel—that most delightful process of laying in store of souvenirs and fair visions. Madame de Staël was unable to get outside of herself and become a mere passive, but extremely sensitive, recipient of perceptions, otherwise she would not have been embarrassed with her own little individuality when she found herself traversing unknown countries where every tree, every plough-boy, and every sound is an object of interest, or contemplating great monuments which have immortalized the names of painters, sculptors, and architects.

Certainly far other thoughts were mine when I jumped out of the train at Milan station, hurriedly deposited my luggage at a hotel, and hailed a cab, saying to the coachman, " Santa Maria delle Grazie." We rode through well-paved narrow streets, between houses whose windows were enveloped in white exterior curtains to keep out the heat ; then we skirted a canal bordered with houses and gardens like the canals in Holland ; here and there through a broad archway we caught a glimpse of the cool court-yards and green trees of the palaces of the rich ; and at last we came to an open square, at one end of which was a brick church, and beside it a white-curtained door over which was the inscription "Cenacolo." Pushing the curtain aside, I paid my franc, passed the turnstile, and there I was in presence of Leonardo da Vinci's famous picture " The Last Supper," the composition of which everybody knows, thanks to Raphael Morghen's excellent engraving. The work is not a fresco painting, but an oil-painting on a plaster surface, occupying the end wall of the refectory of the old convent of St. Mary of the Graces, at the other end of which is a real fresco of the Crucifixion, by Montorfano, dated 1495. This refectory is a lofty, bare Gothic room, at least 100 feet long and about 20 feet broad, with lattice windows away up at the top under the ceiling. The floor is paved with red tiles. The side walls, as well as the ceiling, are whitewashed, except at the two ends where remnants of decorative painting are rapidly peeling off. Over the Leonardo picture are three arched compartments with remains of frescoed armorial bearings; below the picture, in the middle, a bricked-up door cuts into it, and the rest of the wall is simply plastered and colored with a hideous greenish - yellow tint. In front of the picture are a dozen chairs for admirers to sit upon, and half a dozen fearful copies and reconstitutions of the work by Milanese artists, who have carelessly left their visiting-cards on the shelves of their easels to record their shame or to notify their address. In short, this great monument of the genius of Leonardo is exhibited to strangers by the Milanese in the most unfavorable conditions of light and of surroundings, and one wonders what becomes of the thousands of francs which are paid by travellers every year at the turnstile of the " Cenacolo."   Surely some part of this revenue might be devoted to arranging the refectory more decently, or at least to giving to the dirty yellow wall beneath the picture a coat of color of some dark, neutral tint, so that the composition might not suffer from the crude neighborhood of mouldering and leprous whitewash.   Alas! time has been very cruel to Leonardo's vision, and damp and age have spotted it with scabs and scars ; but the hand of man has been still more cruel than time in repainting the faces, hands, and drapery of the figures ; and the injuries of both kinds are only too evident in the violent light that streams in from the windows. " The Last Supper " is only a shadowy remnant of what it was, and yet, in spite of its state of degradation, it requires but a half-closing of the eyes and a slight effort of imagination in order to evoke from the ruin an image of the splendid harmony of color which the work originally must have presented.   Leonardo is essentially the painter of the mysterious and of the ineffable.   His painting has been compared to music in a minor key. His shadows are veils which he thickens or half draws aside to reveal dimly some secret thought, and time, which deteriorates other painting, improves Leonardo's because it deepens the harmonious shadow in which he loves to plunge. The first impression of this picture, when one half closes one's eyes and voluntarily abstracts the white specks where the paint has peeled off and left bare the plaster, is as it were of a dream floating on the surface of the wall. "It is the shade of a painting," said Théophile Gautier, "the spectre of a masterpiece." In the middle of the table is Christ, having on his right St. John, with features of almost feminine delicacy, and on his left Judas, with curly hair, base profile, and finger uplifted in self-disculpation. The disciples, seated or standing along the three sides of the table, are arranged in groups of three, two groups on each side of the Saviour, thus forming the traditional and still superstitiously dreaded thirteen at table. In the coloration, which we may regard as a memorandum of the original, and which we can confirm from an examination of the thirty or forty old copies of "The Last Supper" existing in Italy, France, and Germany, blues and reds predominate on a warm, neutral gray ground. The light comes from the window at the back of the principal figure, and through the opening is seen a crepuscular landscape of green fields, deep blue hills, and a sky paling in the twilight. The impression is one of divine melancholy and tender, harmonious calm—an effect due to the ex-

pression of the head of the Saviour, and to the
calmness of the evening landscape. It will be
remarked that the prodigious composition of
this work is reasoned out in such a manner as to
concentrate our attention first on the figure of the
Saviour and secondly on that of his betrayer ; for
the heads and figures of all the other apostles
are set off against the neutral background of
the wall of the room, while St. John is made to
lean away from Christ in order to leave more of
the distant landscape visible. The silvery blue
light of this calm evening prospect fascinates the
eye at once and leads it to the figure of which
this suave scenery forms, as it were, a tranquil
aureole, namely, the figure of Christ. Next we
notice Judas, over the top of whose head we see
once more the pure, calm sky; and next the luminous horizon line of the distant blue hills
catches our eye, and leads it to the figure of the
beloved disciple, St. John. Then the composition descends at a gentle perspective angle on
each side of the picture, and shows us the other
disciples with animated gestures and expressions,
while familiar objects scattered over the table-
cloth complete the idea of the scene and astonish
us by the delicacy with which, all patches as they
are, they play into the general harmony of this
wonderful masterpiece of human genius. One
cannot conceive anything more beautiful and
more impressive. But remark that what we sincere-

ly admire in this " Last Supper " are only the composition and the impressiveness and animation which are due to the grouped action and to the individual gestures of the figures portrayed; for probably the only fragment of this pseudo-fresco in which the handiwork of Leonardo remains undesecrated by the restorer's brush is the sky and blue landscape seen through the window at the back. Finished in 1498, this picture was already half effaced in 1540, and in 1560 Lomazzo describes it as having lost its color so far that the outlines alone of the figures were still visible. The Carthusian monk Sanese says that there was hardly anything of the picture to be seen in 1624. In 1652 the Dominican fathers had a doorway cut through the centre of the picture, thus sacrificing the legs of the central figures and a part of the table-cloth, as the visitor still sees; and the same Dominicans in 1726 had the whole picture restored by one Bellotti, who, as Stendhal says in his " Histoire de la Peinture en Italie," "dared to repaint in its entirety Vinci's picture, hidden behind a screen of canvas. Afterwards he uncovered the picture and showed it to the stupid monks, who marvelled at the powerfulness of his secret for *reviving* colors. The only portion which he respected was the sky, whose truly divine transparency he seemingly despaired of imitating with his coarse colors. The amusing part of this misadventure," adds Stendhal, "is that the

connoisseurs still continued to praise the grace
and delicacy of Leonardo's brush.   A M. Cochin,
an artist justly esteemed at Paris, found this picture to be very much in the taste of Raphael."
Even nowadays you may still hear visitors going
into ecstasies over the "rich and soft color"
and the "mellow harmony," although the colors
that we now see are not even those of Bellotti,
for the picture was again repainted in 1770 by a
barbarian named Mazza, who began his work by
scraping out what remained of Leonardo's color
with a chimney sweep's iron scraper.   In 1796
some French dragoons who had their quarters in
this refectory amused themselves by "shying"
bricks at the heads of the apostles.   In 1800 an
inundation left a foot of water in the room, and
this water remained there until it evaporated.
The wonder is that, after encountering such a
series of disasters, there should remain of the
original picture even a patch of landscape and
sky and the mutilated and phantom forms of the
figures.

After admiring Leonardo's masterpiece I went
to the famous Ambrosian Library, not only to see
more work by the master, but first of all to see
the color of the hair of Lucrezia Borgia.   The
written documents of history and the graphic
souvenirs of painters and sculptors have bequeathed to us the memories of many women,
whose vanished beauty or whose legendary fasci-

nation haunts our minds and makes us eternally regret the backward limit of life and the impossibility of returning into the limbo of the past. What was she like, this Lucrezia? What was the sound of her voice? What the fascination of her smile? What the majesty of her presence? In these musty and unhandsome rooms of the old Ambrosian Library, in the paltriest glass cases that can be imagined, are exhibited a few of the innumerable treasures of this famous collection, which possesses 100,000 printed books and 15,000 manuscripts. Here is Petrarch's copy of Virgil, a manuscript adorned with miniatures by Memmi, and enriched with marginal notes by Petrarch's "own particular pen," to translate the words of the custode. One of these marginal notes marks the day when the poet saw Laura for the first time in the church of Saint Claire at Avignon, the 6th April, 1327. At the same hour, on the same date, the 6th April, 1348, Laura died, and Petrarch wrote these words on the margin of his favorite book, which no longer interested him: "Ut scilicet nihil esse debere quod amplius mihi placeat in hâc vitâ."

Close to Petrarch's Virgil is one of the ten autograph letters of Lucrezia Borgia which the Ambrosian possesses. It is written on a small quarto sheet of paper yellowed with age, and in firm, upright cursive characters, resembling those of old manuscripts. This letter was addressed to him

who became afterwards Cardinal Bembo, and to
it the gracious lady attached a lock of her beautiful, sunny, golden hair.   I remember that, in his
correspondence with the publisher Murray, Byron
confesses to have stolen *one single hair* from this
lock ; and I presume that it was this larceny on the
part of his lordship which caused the curators of
the Ambrosian to detach the hair from the letter, and to put it, for greater security, in a common card-board box with a glass top—a most paltry receptacle, utterly unworthy of such a precious treasure.   I copied the letter, with its quaint
abbreviations, but, as for translating it, our English language has not the suppleness and im-
measurable prettiness of expression necessary to
give the equivalent sense of the epistle of this
gracious lady to her " Misser Pietro mio."   In
substance she acknowledges a letter from Bembo,
thanks him for some verses, sends him some
verses in return written with her own hand, and
signs :

" De Ferrara a di xxviiij de marzo.
Desiderosa gratificarvi
Lucretia Esten . . de Borgia."

The whole tone of the letter is that of mere
friendship, but there was added that fulgurant
lock of golden hair, enough to enflame the soul
of an anchorite.

Another pearl of the Ambrosian Library, two
pages of which alone are niggardly shown to the

public, is a huge folio of 400 pages, called the " Codice Atlantico," which contains the observations of the painter Leonardo da Vinci on mechanics, hydraulics, optics, fortification, geometry, and engineering, the whole accompanied by 1700 drawings by the hand of the master, and by text written from right to left, after the manner of the Orientals.   Leonardo was a universal genius, who anticipated Newton and Bacon, invented the camera obscura, and was the first geologist who maintained the theory that most continents once formed the bed of the sea.   All this has been read in Leonardo's Book of Machines by savants who have taken the trouble to decipher the text.

The picture-gallery attached to the Ambrosian Library is very rich in drawings by Leonardo, and especially in caricatures, which the artist used to make in the Borghetto on market days.   But both the show-cases in the library and the exhibition rooms in the museum are in a sad state of neglect, and all the precious pictures and rarities are presented in the most miserable conditions of arrangement, light, and preservation.   In the library the few manuscripts exhibited are crowded pell-mell in the paltriest show-cases, and that famous lock of Lucrezia Borgia's hair is kept in a mean pink paper box such as those you see in the Japanese stores containing toy spiders and sensitive bugs.   The disorder of the museum is comparable only to the confusion of a badly kept bric-à-brac store, and the pictures are hung on the walls, anyhow, nameless and numberless, good, bad, and indifferent, in the paltriest old fly-blown frames imaginable. Here is a lovely Botticelli of immense value stuck all awry in a frame which is struggling to part company with the picture. Here are scores of drawings by Leonardo, by Albert Dürer, by Luini, by Verrochio, stuck up in big cases in the wildest medley, originals, copies, genuine and attributed drawings, all together. Such barbarous and neglectful keeping of precious works is unworthy of the civilized and progressive town that Milan professes to be.

The Milan Museum, or Brera Gallery, is better arranged in well-lighted rooms, and one can admire in comparative visual comfort Raphael's "Sposalizio," Leonardo's crayon and sanguine head of Christ, a study for the "Last Supper," remarkable works by Crivelli, Tintoretto, Mantegna, and above all by Luini, many of whose frescoes have been removed from churches and convents and placed here in security. But even here is plenty of room for improvement, re-hanging, re-framing, and re-arranging. Imagine that these Luini frescoes, the gems of the collection, are hung mostly in a corridor where they receive only reflected light. The modern Italians are skillful in building prisons and barracks and armor-plated ships, but they have hitherto devot-

ed no attention to building model museums with
a view to adequately preserving and well display-
ing the masterpieces which they have inherited
from their glorious ancestors.   Luini's frescoes
ought to occupy the place of honor in this Brera
Gallery, for he is a great master of ingenuous ex-
pressiveness, grace, elegance, and *naïveté*, a most
exquisite and human artist.   I know of nothing
in sacred imagery more pure, more virginal, more
sincere, and more joyfully impressive than Luini's
picture of the three angels lifting Saint Catherine
out of her tomb and carrying her up to heaven.
How touching in its simplicity and how direct the
fresco of the three maidens in a field playing at hot
cockles!   And who are these maidens?   Evidently in Luini's mind one is the Virgin and the other
two are her companions, and the flowery, pale-
green meadow may, if you please, be supposed to
be just outside Nazareth.   Raphael's "Sposalizio"
is certainly graceful and consummate, but how
much more charming, how much more human,
how much more suave and poetic is Luini's fresco of this same subject of the marriage of Joseph.
In all Luini's frescoes, both at Milan and elsewhere, there is a peculiar charm in the peasant
figures, in the incidents of rustic life, and in the
summary visions of sweet landscape which he always introduces in his religious scenes, so win-
ning and unsophisticated in sentiment, and so
blond, so luminous, and so distinguished in tone.

Some of the finest pictures in Milan are in the
Poldi-Pezzoli Museum, a modern foundation of a
kind of which we may hope some day or other to
see several in America. The Chevalier Gian
Giacomo Poldi-Pezzoli, founder of the museum,
died in 1879 and bequeathed to the town of Milan
his house just as it was when he lived in it, together with all its contents, and an annuity to
pay the cost of its maintenance. The chevalier
had devoted his whole life to forming a collection
of pictures, furniture, stuffs and tapestries, arms,
bronzes, porcelain, enamels, glass, and miscellaneous objects of art, and to lodging the same
in a house worthy of such treasures. The Poldi-
Pezzoli collection has been left just as its owner
arranged it, as the chief ornament of a gentleman's dwelling. The house is very luxuriously
arranged, and interesting as a specimen of a fine
modern Italian dwelling. I do not say that it is
a model of style. On the contrary, the chevalier,
who seems to have had excellent taste in pictures,
appears to have allowed a florid nineteenth-century decorator to run wild in the adornment of
his rooms, which are over-loaded with carving,
gilding, stucco-work, and wood mosaic. But in
this house are some prodigious marvels of art,
especially about two hundred pictures by the old
masters, of which none are bad, while a dozen
are beyond praise or estimation, notably a Luini,
representing the Angel Raphael bringing little

Toby home to his parents, a Virgin and Child by Botticelli, more exquisite even than the Botticelli in the Louvre at Paris, a portrait of a lady by Pier della Francesca, a Perugino, and a Crivelli. I cannot say how delightful it is to contemplate masterpieces in surroundings such as the Poldi-Pezzoli mansion affords, each work displayed in a perfect light, isolated sufficiently, and yet always in the neighborhood of beautiful objects, so that when the eye does quit unwillingly the fascinating beauty of an angel face, or the splendor of one of those gorgeously enthroned Virgins which the proud painter signed in letters of gold on a slab of *lapis lazuli*

·:·KAROLVS·:·CHRIVELLVS·:·VENETVS·:·EQVES·:: LAVREATVS·:·PINXIT·:·

it may turn to a graven crystal vase, a rich enamel, or a perspective of green foliage seen through the open window, instead of being met by the ungraceful form of a vulgar spit-box as is generally the case in the galleries of a regular museum. The example of the Chevalier Poldi-Pezzoli is one which the American millionaire collectors would do well to meditate and follow.

The monument which blind tradition and the pride of the Milanese make out to be the most splendid in the city, if not one of the wonders of the world, I mean the Duomo or Cathedral, is the one which least struck me and about which I have least to say. It is the largest church in the world next to St. Peter's in Rome; it is built entirely of white marble, both inside and out, and even the roof is made of marble slabs; the outside walls and the roof and pinnacles are peopled by six thousand seven hundred and sixteen marble statues, enough to populate a town. From the outside the Duomo looks like a glacier with its thousand needles sculptured and fretted into elegant forms; or like some fairy Alcazar, bordered with lace work, set against the sky and surmounted by a forest of pinnacles and turrets and pointed shafts, on which are balanced in mid air statues of saints. All this is very wonderful and very enormous, but from an architectural point of view, the only point of view to be taken in considering an architectural monument, the Duomo of Milan is a huge, glittering Gothic toy, the biggest marble gewgaw in the world, over-decorated, impure in style, pretentious and without interest, structurally, because everywhere this stupendous *tour de force* has to be held together by iron braces and clamps. The story runs that the two architects who began the church in the middle of the sixteenth century, Pelligrino Tibaldi and Martino Bassi, were always at loggerheads, Bassi protesting constantly against Tibaldi's plans. The differences of the two rival architects were referred successively to the arbitration of Palladio, Vasari, and Vignole, of whom the latter, when consulted on a question of supporting iron braces, sided with Bassi and emitted the excellent axiom: "An edifice ought not to need being held by leading strings." This is the best and most comprehensive criticism that has been made of the Cathedral of Milan.

There are innumerable churches and convents of more or less interest at Milan, but in travelling it is a wise thing to remain content with fine and capital impressions, and to neglect secondary curiosities. There is nothing special to be said about busy modern Milan, with its innumerable two-cent horse-cars and its universal use of electric light. It is a rich, clean, ostentatious, and gay city, where there are no curb-stones, where the draymen eat iced cream in cafés, and where the patron saint, Saint Charles Borromeo, is considered to be mightier than God himself.

WHAT a degenerate race we moderns are, is the thought which is constantly recurring as one wanders about the old Italian towns, admiring the remnants of past splendor, the palaces where the old seigneurs passed their magnificent and often criminal existences, the churches where they are buried with all the pomp of art and epigraphic eloquence, the streets where they promenaded, each followed by a battling retinue. Of all the old European towns that I have seen Verona most completely retains its mediæval aspect; houses, palaces, churches remain just as they were in the days of the Capulets and the Montagues; and if Dante's host, Can Grande Scaliger, were to come back to this world he would find his palace looking much as it looked when he was lord, and when he invited Giotto to come and paint his apartments in fresco. Time has devoured Giotto's frescoes, and Can Grande would doubtless be astonished to find that the fact of his having given hospitality to the poet Dante has done more towards immortalizing his name than all his exploits and bravery as captain-general of the Ghibellines.

But so it is; the events of history are forgotten; the memory of man is too weary to retain the names of a hundred captains; the incidents of the past lose their interest, but the art of the past never appeals in vain to the eye, and the great captains who have protected art and letters are protected in turn by art and letters, and immortalized not so much as great captains but as art patrons. Who cares nowadays about the Guelphs and the Ghibellines, about the feuds of the Scaligers and the Viscontis, or about the hatreds of the Capulets and the Montagues? We only remember them because Dante and Shakespeare have incidentally immortalized them; and the white marble panel which the modern Veronese have placed on the façade of Can Grande's house in the Piazza dei Signori records principally the fact that the exiled Dante found hospitality under this roof. It is indeed in this tragic town of Verona that Dante murmured his verses on exile; it was in this old gray palace that he was the guest of the magnificent Seigneur della Scala, Can Grande, who kept up a literary court in his dwelling; it was here that Dante finally found that the bread of a stranger is bitter, and complained how difficult it was to mount the staircase of another, an allusion doubtless to the name of his host della Scala, Scala meaning in Italian "ladder" or "staircase."

Every step you take in Verona seems to bring

you face to face with some historical souvenir ;
the civilizations of the Romans, of the Middle
Ages, and of the Renaissance have left splendid
traces, and so many are the objects of interest
that you hardly know with which to begin. Under the walls of Verona Marius conquered the
Cimbri, and Vitellius was beaten by Vespasian.
Then came the butcheries of the barbarians, and
Odoacer was crushed by Theodoric. Later
Charlemagne besieged Didier in Verona and took
it by assault. Afterwards came the family feuds
of the Middle Ages. Here indeed is a fine canvas on which to arrange the drama of one's
souvenirs.

Let us begin by a visit to Juliet's house, "la
casa di Giulietta," as the Veronese call it. It is
situated in the very centre of the mediæval town,
in the Via di Capello, on the left-hand side as you
leave the market place, or Piazza dell' Erbe, which
was at once the market and the forum of the old
republic. Imagine a narrow, stuffy street lined
with antique houses, among which is noticeable a
red brick façade with arched Roman windows,
some of which retain remnants of architectural
decoration. On the third flat is a stone balcony
half broken away and resting on huge stone con-
soles. The façade is divided into two by a big
water pipe, and the windows, irregularly distribut-
ed, are hung with rags and other evidences of
poor tenantry. On the ground floor is the shop

of a baker, with the sign "Paneficio Fratelli Tre-
naghi," and the immense archway which gives entrance to the Capulet house.   Over this archway
swings a sign of a cardinal's red hat, and above it
are the words " Al capello, stallo," that is to say
"The Hat Stables;" other signs on the archway
say "Noleggio cavalli," "Horses to hire," and
repeat "Nel capello, stallo."   The house bears
the numbers 19, 21, 23, 25, and over the archway
is a slab of marble, with the following inscription :

> " Queste furono le case dei Capuletti
>   d'onde usci la Giulietta
>   per cui tanto piansero i cuori gentili
>   e i poeti cantarono.
>   Secoli 13 e 14 e V."

Beneath the archway the passage slopes up, and
you enter a vast courtyard, the four sides of which
are occupied by miserable buildings terraced with
rough wooden balconies, on which linen is spread
to dry and to absorb the perfumes of this most
foul-smelling spot.   On each balcony is built a
wooden shed on which is written the word " Cessi "
which means water-closet ; the staircases are
black holes thick with dirt; the courtyard is
crowded with carts and vehicles of all kinds and
redolent of ammoniacal smells ; and next to the stables is a " Caffé Trattoria," a café and a restaurant
where you can be lodged for the night.   Over
this filthy and stinking courtyard, enthroned in a
flourishing vine plant, an image of the Virgin

presides at one end, while at the other end, on the back façade of Juliet's house, are carved in low relief the speaking arms of the Capulets or Capelletti, namely, a hat, or "Capello." And it was here that Juliet had her garden; here that Romeo climbed her balcony; here that the two lovers poured out their souls, until they were surprised by the song of the lark, and the dawn warned them that they must part. This is the house; there can be no doubt about it; and we can imagine the Capulets and their retainers swaggering out of this vast courtyard and down under the archway to the street, ready to fall foul of those hated Montagues. But where was Juliet's balcony?

After visiting Juliet's house, one naturally visits her so-called tomb, "Tomba Giulietta," apocryphal as it may be. On the right bank of the Adige, in the Vicolo Franceschine, at the end of a blind alley, is a white gable pierced by two windows with red shutters and a big green door. On the gable is the inscription "Tomba Giulietta." You pull very hard at the bell-wire, and after waiting five or ten minutes, while the pulling gets transmitted to some very distant bell, the green door wicket opens mysteriously, and you find yourself in a dark passage full of agricultural machinery. At the end of this passage is a vast garden which used to be a Franciscan cemetery. A broad walk, overarched with trailing vines, leads through the garden and gradually develops into a bowling-alley. Finally it turns to the right, and at the end, in a corner of the garden, is a sort of chapel of recent construction, where a woman stands with the inevitable keys waiting to show the sight and to receive a " tip." Inside the chapel is a large red Verona marble trough, at the bottom of which is a cavity " scooped out for the head," and at the opposite end a hole " bored to let in air "—so says the old woman. It was in this marble sepulchre, we are told, that Juliet was laid after she had taken Friar Lawrence's narcotic, and it was here that Romeo saw her. Where she was really buried after she died is not recorded. Scattered around this sarcophagus or trough are fragments of columns and marble. The bottom of the sarcophagus is strewn with a thickness of several inches of visiting-cards; on the wall also are pinned up visiting-cards, mostly bearing Anglo-Saxon names ; and on the wall over the sarcophagus is hung a faded wreath with a card pinned on to it. This card bears the name of an English gentleman, Mr. Talbot Shakspeare, who is less famous than his homonym William. Also pinned on the wall are faded yellow cuttings from a local paper, the *Adige*, giving an account of this tomb, and some photographs which the guardian tries to sell in order to augment her meagre income. Just as we arrived at this classic spot the old woman finished a good stroke of business:

she concluded a transfer of twenty-two photographs of the tomb to the twenty-two members of a "personally conducted" party from Chicago and thereabouts, who were doing Verona in twenty-four hours under the command of a scraggy German boy who directed their movements by the shrill blasts of a pea-whistle. These worthy people, men, women, and children, seemed to appreciate Juliet's tomb, and I heard some of them express satisfaction at its bigness. It certainly is big, but, if the truth were known, I am afraid it would turn out to be neither Juliet's tomb, nor yet a tomb at all, but simply a big marble fountain basin such as you see used all over Southern Europe for washing purposes. It is a trough or *lavoir*, and the hole pierced "to let air in" was rather pierced to let the water out. Thirty years ago, when Charles Blanc saw this so-called "tomb of Juliet," it was still being used as a washing trough by the peasants who owned it. The modern chapel, the broken columns, and all the other paraphernalia date, I suspect, only from the time when "personally conducted" tours were first organized by certain inventive and useful citizens whose names are well-known all over the world. Still it must be admitted that the tradition is not entirely modern. This supposed tomb was shown to travellers in the beginning of this century, and the archduchess Marie Louise of Parma had a bracelet made of fragments of the stone. This

11

detail is given by Chateaubriand in his memoirs.
At the time of the Congress of Verona, Chateaubriand dined at the house of the archduchess,
saw this bracelet, and was told the history of it by
the wearer.

One of the grandest curiosities of Verona is
the old Roman arena, or amphitheatre, built in
the third century of our era. and now still in excellent preservation with the exception of the
outer wall, of which four arcades alone remain
standing. Here indeed is a monument which
must make the moderns feel small. With our
present theatres, holding our two or three thousand people, we are in danger of being burned to
death, and the exit is a process as perilous as it is
long. Here is a theatre where 22,000 people
could be seated comfortably, and where every
300 spectators had a separate staircase and entrance door. The exterior arrangement of this
edifice can be readily imagined from the fragment
which remains intact: it presented three super-
posed rows of arches, very massive and of a rustic
Doric style. The lowest row contains 72 arches,
each of which was a door for entrance and exit,
communicating with the broad interior circuit
from which the staircases start leading to the amphitheatre. A second interior circuit communi-
cates with the dens for the wild beasts and the
rooms of the gladiators. At each end of the
arena are the galleries for the authorities, and

the seats mount up, row above row, from the arena to the sky, 43 rows. The arena measures 230 feet long and 135 feet broad, and the outside circumference of the whole edifice is about 1500. So far as concerns the amphitheatre proper, the seats and the arena, the edifice is in perfect preservation, repairs having been made whenever necessary ever since the fourteenth century; indeed, a performance was actually given there not so very long ago, when all the sovereigns and diplomatists were assembled on the occasion of the Congress of Verona. Chateaubriand relates that fossil Verona had not enough inhabitants to fill the building, and that press-gangs were sent out to collect spectators from the surrounding villages. This wonderful and gigantic mass of masonry is built of hewn stone, brick, and rubble. The tone which age has given to the exterior walls is roseate red, paling into gray and dull white.

The great charm of Verona is that it has retained its mediæval aspect. There are no modern buildings and no modern improvements, except a tramway and a few very discreet gas-lights. The café of Verona, which, of course, bears the name of Victor Emmanuel, is established in a magnificent palace, that of the Sparavieri, built by Sammicheli, who was the Palladio of Verona, and who adorned the town with innumerable palaces, and at the same time strengthened it with fortresses and bastions with embrasures such as Leonardo da Vinci designed in his Book of Machines in the Ambrosian Library. Sammicheli was a wonderful man, and, at the risk of re-discovering America, I venture particularly to recommend him to the attention of architects and house-builders who may not happen to be familiar with his work. Legend says that he was the personal friend of Paul Veronese, and that it was he who designed the fine architectural backgrounds which form such a conspicuous feature in Veronese's pictures. However that may be, Sammicheli built half a dozen palaces at Verona which are models of rich domestic architecture. These are the palaces which bear the names Bevilacqua, Canossa, Pompei, Guasta-Versa, Maffei, and Portalupi, elegant and majestic buildings enriched with the most exquisite detail. The Palazzo del Consiglio, commonly called the Loggia, on the Piazza dei Signori, is one of the most beautiful early Renaissance buildings in northern Italy, most richly decorated and most perfectly proportioned. Verona is admirably calculated to disperse our modern ascetic ideas about banishing color from architecture and sculpture. The façade of this Loggia is all aglow with colored marbles and gilded capitals. In the neighboring market-place, or Piazza dell' Erbe, the façades of the quaint old houses are covered with frescoes painted by pupils of Mantegna and by Paul Veronese when he was a young man. In every narrow street you see houses decorated with now faded frescoes, balconies sculptured into the loveliest fret-work of stone, doors gorgeous with bronze knockers of splendid design, trefoliated windows, door-posts chiselled with ornaments that the pencil alone can render, street-corners crowned with statues, arcades decorated with colored bas-reliefs in stone or terra-cotta—a profusion of color and ornament which words cannot describe. In the churches the splendor of ornament and color is still greater, and that, too, not merely in the added richness of pictures, bronzes, statuary, and wood-carving, but in the very structure of the buildings, composed of bricks of various colors intermingled with stone and marble and terra-cotta. For the architect, the decorator, the scene-painter, and the searcher after the picturesque and the romantic, Verona is a mine of wealth, an inspiration. The palaces, the two churches of Saint Zeno and Saint Anastasia, and the Piazza dei Signori are monuments which will never be forgotten when once they have been seen.

The Piazza dei Signori is surrounded by material and other souvenirs of the famous della Scala or Scaligers who were seigneurs of Verona in the Middle Ages. When you are seated at the Café Dante, in the middle of the Piazza, with the pigeons picking up the crumbs at your feet, you can run over the history of the city and point to

the spots where many a famous event took place.
On your left is the Loggia and the palace of Can
Grande; through the archway at the corner is
the church of Santa Maria Antica and the tombs
of the Scaligers; forming the angle of the square
is another Scaliger palace with brick battlements;
separated from this palace by an archway is the
tribunal with severe barred windows; on the other
side of the square a beautiful old well dated 1478
and surmounted by delicate Corinthian columns;
and hard by the Volto Barbaro, an archway beneath which Mastino I. della Scala was assassi-
nated in the twelfth century. All the houses and
buildings in this square are old—three, four, five,
and six hundred years old; the only really modern
element in the square is the statue of Dante which
stands on a pedestal in the middle, opposite the
door of that Scaliger palace where he found the
bread so bitter. The very pavement of huge
stone slabs is the same that Dante trod. In the
neighboring church of Santa Maria Antica, Can
Grande and his literary and artistic court used to
go to hear mass. And now, in the little square
in front of this church, all these Scaligers, several
of whom were assassins and scoundrels, lie at rest
in the proudest and most beautiful Gothic tombs
in Europe, each one surrounded by angels of
marble and lace-work curtains of wrought iron
that seem to have been designed and forged by
fairy fingers. So calm, so ancient, so complete

is the aspect of these monuments that one could readily believe one's self transported back to the days of Giotto, and one is quite surprised to see people pass who wear melon hats and tweed trousers, and who never lift their heads to look at the statues of illustrious sons of Verona which adorn the cornice of the old Council Palace: Pliny the younger, Catullus, Vitruvius the architect, Emilius Macer, the poet and friend of Virgil, and Cornelius Nepos, whose limpid style used to seem so stupid when we were obliged to read it in school on fine summer afternoons.

THE chief attraction of travelling is surprise produced by something novel and unforeseen. As I approached Venice, I wished never to have seen the pictures of Canaletto, or the water-colors of Bonington and Ziem. The descriptions of writers, even of the precise and brilliant Théophile Gautier, leave some margin to the imagination; but where the painter and the photographer have passed, the impression loses at least its fine feather-edge of newness and crispness. And yet, when we left the iron road and set foot in a gondola, and when this gondola began to glide along the Grand Canal, rocking regularly, turning corners, making hair-breadth escapes of collisions, winding in and out through the inextricable network and infinite capillarity of the aquatic streets of Venice, our astonishment was as great as if we had never read a book about Venice, and never seen a Canaletto or a Ziem. The movement of the gondola is delightful in the extreme, and surpassed only in suavity by the movement of a "caïque" on the Bosphorus. On the other hand, the gondola itself is a sufficiently funereal craft;

the gondolier is an unromantic person who rarely
sings, and whose dress is commonplace; the
canals of Venice are decidedly foul-smelling, and
the palaces with which they are lined are approaching a sad state of ruination. Travellers
rarely quit the emphatic tone in describing what
they have seen, even when the things they mention are mediocre; the idea being, I suppose, that
it would compromise a traveller's reputation to
admit that he had seen something which was not
worth seeing. In real truth one of the nuisances
of travelling is that, on the recommendation of
the guide-books, we are constantly going to see
some stupid thing or other which in our normal
state of existence would not captivate our attention for a single moment. People rave about the
entrance to Venice by the Grand Canal : the entrance to Lyons by the Rhone, or to Paris by the
Seine, is certainly more grandiose. The marvel
of Venice is not the Grand Canal, it is the Piazzetta, St. Mark's, and the Ducal Palace seen from
the sea ; it is the essential queerness of the town,
where you cannot take two steps without arriving
at a canal or a bridge, and where from year's end
to year's end you never see a larger four-footed
animal than a dog or a cat. The Piazza San
Marco is the realization of a fairy tale ; neither
Canaletto nor Gautier, nor any painter or writer
can give an adequate representation of this wonderful sight. On two sides are the monumental

structures of the Procuraties; to the right the Campanile rises 300 feet in the air; to the left is the clock-tower, surmounted by automatic bronze giants holding hammers upraised ready to strike the hours; in the background is St. Mark's Church, with its leaden domes shining as if they were of silver, its five porches with their splendor of mosaics on gold ground, its three or four hundred columns of porphyry, granite, serpentine, vert antique, and Pentelic marble; its bronze horses, its undulating silhouette fringed with gold angels intermingled with fantastic vegetation of snow-white marble. In front of the church rise three red flag-poles, shod with beautiful bronze pedestals; while at the right-hand corner you catch a glimpse of the windows of the Ducal Palace, with its walls of white and rose marble.

This vision is a marvel only approached in splendor by the vision of the Ducal Palace, St. Mark's, and the Piazzetta seen from the sea. From every point of view the scene is one of marvellous richness, marred only by the degenerate humanity which animates it. Modern Venice is a dead city, living on the curiosity and gullibility of foreign visitors. You cannot go near St. Mark's or the Ducal Palace without being pestered by the offers of guides and photograph-sellers, who buzz around you like flies. And all the arcades around St. Mark's Place are occupied by little shops, where are sold the trashiest, paltriest, and most abominable jewelry, trinkets, knick-knacks, and souvenirs which it is possible to imagine ; and the shopkeepers stand at their doors and solicit you, first in one tongue and then in another, for the wretches sell their rubbish in all languages. This St. Mark's Place, the scene of the above-mentioned splendors and inconveniences, is the centre of Venetian life. In the arcades are four cafés, of which the most famous is the Café Florian, renowned for its excellent coffee during the past hundred years. Towards sunset, these four cafés occupy two thirds of the vast square with their little tables and chairs, leaving only a passage free down the middle ; and on the four or five nights a week when the military band plays every chair is taken, and the crowd remains thick until midnight. All Venice is there, rich and poor alike, but more poor than rich. All the visitors are there ; and everybody who has a sixpence in his pocket is eating ices and *granitas*, which are excellent in Venice, and only surpassed by those of Milan. Amid the crowd circulate two or three flower-girls, daintily dressed *à la Parisienne;* hardworking men and boys, who try to sell their halfpenny papers, *Corriere della Sera, Venezia, Adriatico;* and the caramel-vendor, who offers grapes, plums, and quarters of oranges *glacés* with sugar and skewered on sticks of white wood. A degenerate crowd, indeed, ill-favored and uncomely withal. Where are the blonde

Venetian women that Palma Vecchio and Titian depicted? Where are all the gay and graceful follies of the Venice which Longhi has immortalized in his delicate paintings? Where are the swaggering and brilliantly dressed gondoliers whom we see in Carpaccio's pictures? United Italy and Manchester wares have put an end to all this. Gay and brilliant Venice is only a memory, and a penny steamboat, smoking and hideous, now runs up and down that Grand Canal where formerly the gilded gondolas of the Republic, and the still richer gondolas of the ambassadors, were towed up and down in stately pomp, for the gondoliers of the Republic were too grand personages to work. They were clad in mantles of red velvet embroidered with gold, and wore large caps *à l'Albanoise*, which made them so proud that they could not condescend to handle an oar, but stood up bravely on the gondolas of the Republic and had themselves towed by small boats, with musicians on board to play and charm their ears.

Venice has been written about so much and so enthusiastically that one forms perhaps too great ideas about it before having seen the reality. It must be admitted that there has been much romancing done, on the part of Byron especially, and not a little on the part of George Sand and Gautier. Doubtless, on account of the souvenirs it calls up, Venice is a most interesting place; its narrow streets are most curious; its canals, its gondolas, even its gondoliers, most romantic and delightful. But, in sober truth, all that one needs to see of Venice is the general aspect, St. Mark's Church and Place, the Ducal Palace, and the pictures in the Accademia. If you go off to this church and that *scuola*, trying to feel at second-hand the ethico-æsthetic sensations of John Ruskin; or if you go to the prisons of the Ducal Palace, or to the shores of the Lido, with a view to treading in the footsteps of Byron, you are doomed to disappointment. The prisons of the Ducal Palace are very comfortable apartments, and the Lido is a barren island, on which an enterprising company has established a very prosperous bathing establishment and seaside restaurant, thirty cents there and back, bath and towels included —a sort of Venetian Coney Island. The Lido is also the Jewish burying-ground.

Yet one may well spend a week in Venice, and explore the town thoroughly, even at the cost of numerous disappointments, amply compensated for by the indelible souvenirs of the Piazza San Marco, of the sea-view, and of the pictures by Carpaccio, John Bellini, Titian, Paris Bordone, and Paul Veronese, which are the pearls of the Academy. Nevertheless, far from being a fairy city, Venice is a mouldering, decayed, and decrepit old place, and (there is no use in disguising the fact) it smells abominably — all these canals being, of course, tidal, and rising and sinking with the waters of the Adriatic.

In the city famous for mortadella, I lodged in an inn which was formerly a palace—a vast and magnificent house, built around a courtyard surrounded by arcades, and enlivened with the luxuriant verdure of immense oleander-trees in pots. I have a charming souvenir of this Hôtel Brun, where, with the thermometer at 93°, I was able to sit in the shade under the arcades, and sip exquisite, savory coffee, and contemplate a patch of lapis-lazuli blue sky framed in arches and architectural lines, which reminded me of the sumptuous and luminous backgrounds of the pictures of Paul Veronese. In the late afternoon, when the thermometer at last sank to 90°, I ventured to inspect the town. All the streets in Bologna are bordered by arcades, convenient enough as shelter against sun and rain, but monotonous in the end, because they transform the streets into long cloisters, absorb the light, and give the town a cold and monastic aspect. Unromantic as the remark may seem, I must state that the first thing which struck me in Bologna was the rarity of shops for the sale of mortadella

and the multiplicity of barbers' tonsorial saloons,
all open to the street, so that the ragged urchins
may regale themselves with the sight of soaped
chins and bald crowns. Never within such a
limited space have I seen so many barbers, and
my curiosity was all the more lively because I
noticed that the Bolognese are a bearded race.
The phenomenon appeared so strange that I determined to try one of these Figaros, and to question him adroitly, and so gather knowledge. The
explanation he gave me was satisfactory: the
Bolognese wear beards because they are shopkeepers and functionaries; but the principal cus-
tomers of the barbers are the country-people and
peasants, who are a shaven race, and who come
into the town to sell their produce and to get their
chins scraped *secundum artem*. After thanking
the barber for his information and for his lightness of hand, I wandered along arcades until I
came to a square where two leaning towers have
tottered now for many centuries without falling:
one is called the Torre degli Asinelli, 300 feet high
and strongly resembling a Manchester chimney;
the other is the Torre Garisenda, built in 1110,
with an inclination of 9 feet from the perpendicular. This tower is only 150 feet high, but it has
the honor of having suggested a metaphor to
Dante.

Coffee at the café on the Piazza Vittorio Emmanuele was the natural conclusion of this first

promenade in Bologna ; and the view of Jean de Bologna's colossal fountain of Neptune and of the quaint, yellow, castellated Municipal Palace was a consolatory spectacle, which carried one away back to the thirteenth century, when the building was constructed. The next morning I visited the churches, finding in them nothing very marvellous; and next I sought the picture-gallery, where Guido, the three Carracci, Domenichino, and Albano reign supreme, the glory of the Bolognese school. This gallery looks as neglected and uncared-for as most public galleries in Italy, and the conditions of exhibition are as bad as they can be. The Bologna Gallery has, for instance, a beautiful set of engravings by Albert Dürer, signed with his monogram, and yet most of them are ticketed with the word "anonymous." Imagine the state of mind of the curator of a State museum who is unable to recognize the work of Albert Dürer. Among the very old pictures I discovered a portrait of the Madonna, on a gold ground, in the style of the primitives, signed by, I presume, the first lady-artist in Europe, Catterina Vigri, called the Saint of Bologna, "La Santa di Bologna." Catterina was born in 1413 and died in 1463. Afterwards Bologna became quite a place for lady-artists, among whom Lavinia di Bologna and Elizabetta Sirani became especially famous. Elizabetta painted quite as good or quite as bad religious pictures as Guido Reni.

The reputed "pearl" of the Bologna Gallery is Raphael's "Saint Cecilia "—by no means a pearl, for it is not remarkable for charm of color, for harmony of composition, or for clearness of signification. It is a poor Raphael, painted to order for some church or cloister, or for some confraternity whose devotion demanded the anachronistic juxtaposition of Saint Paul, Saint John, and Saint Cecilia in the same picture. The great Italian painters were constantly hampered by similar orders, and the museums of Europe are full of the sad results.

From Bologna to Ravenna is a four hours' journey, by slow trains and branch lines, across a flat country not well reputed for healthiness. Formerly a port of the Adriatic and the capital of the Gothic kings, and subsequently the residence of the exarch, or lieutenant, of the Eastern emperors, Ravenna is now nearly six miles distant from the sea, and as dead as a country town can be with 12,000 inhabitants and no commerce in particular. Chance having caused me to arrive at Ravenna in the evening, all that could be done was to sup and then seek out the principal café of the town. With the aid of a map and of topographical instinct, I passed through some sombre and mysterious streets, and reached safely the Café Vittorio Emmanuele, situated, of course, on the Piazza Vittorio Emmanuele. Opposite the café was an old palace converted into barracks;

to the left the Town Hall, with a vast luminous dial in the clock-tower; to the right two tall granite columns, erected by the Venetians in 1483, says the guide-book, and now covered with electioneering placards; beyond, a brick portico built on very ancient granite columns, and, under the portico, shops without fronts, yawning caverns flashing out their light into the general obscurity of the square. And in the moonlight this square and its surrounding buildings look like some romantic stage scenery, and one might indulge in all kinds of dreams were one not recalled to reality by the voice of the newsboy crying "*Il Secolo*," and by the sound of clinking spoons and cups produced by the Ravennese taking their ice-cream or their evening moka. But, in spite of the high civilization of the Café Vittorio Emmanuele, and although the ladies are dressed *à la Parisienne*, Ravenna is essentially a place to dream in, and everything you see carries you back in imagination at least a thousand years. The great monuments of Ravenna date from the fifth to the eighth centuries, and there is no place, not even Rome, where primitive Christian art can be so well studied. The two churches of St. Apollinaris, the church of St. Vitalis, the baptistery and the mausoleum of the Empress Galla Placida, all decorated with mosaics twelve and thirteen hundred years old, are the most wonderfully preserved specimens of ecclesiastical architecture and deco-

ration that can be seen, not excepting even St. Sophia at Constantinople, which served as the model
for St. Vitalis. No description, no photograph, no
painting can give an adequate idea of the style,
color, and effect of these immense wall-covering
mosaic pictures and ornaments, very different
from those in St. Mark's at Venice. One must
make the journey in order to obtain the impression. Three full days spent in the contemplation
of the mosaics, in the study of the architecture,
and in the examination in the museum of the most
interesting specimens of the artistic productions
of the centuries which preceded that of Charlemagne, were not too long, even for a lay observer,
and I started at last for Florence reluctantly,
fearing that I might have missed something
which I ought to have seen. But is not the path
of the traveller always paved with regrets ?

CERTAINLY it is warm in Italy in the summer, and during my last month's wanderings the day temperature has varied between 95° and 100° Fahrenheit. But if one can endure this heat without inconvenience one is rewarded by the aspect of the country in the full exuberance of its verdant fertility. I cannot imagine anything more beautiful than the summer aspect of Florence and of its surrounding hills and valleys seen from the terraces of the Boboli Gardens or from the heights of San Miniato or Fiesole. It is a spectacle that appeals to the thoughts as much as to the eye, for before us is a soil which has had the rare privilege of nurturing two civilizations. The fields which stretch away between the river and the Apennines still hide beneath their surface the vestiges of one of the oldest and noblest civilizations in the world, that of the Etruscans. The beautiful valley of the Arno is before us, irrigated, planted, fertilized, protected against the violence of winds and water, such as it was formed by the industrious hands of the Florentines of the Renaissance. The olive-tree, with its black, gnarled trunk and its pale foliage, gives to the landscape a grave, impressive, and gentle aspect, in keeping with its illustrious history. A multitude of sinuous roads, bordered with cypress and evergreen oaks, connect together villages, orchards, farms, and scattered houses half concealed behind festooning vines. Beyond is Florence seated on either bank of the Arno, over which stretch bridges of various epochs: the Ponte Vecchio still lined with jewellers' shops, the Ponte alla Carraja, the Trinity Bridge, and the bridge with a beautiful name, the Ponte alle Grazie. Within quite a small circuit is the City of Flowers, with its domes, its battlemented towers, its campaniles, its vast arcades, or *loggie*, its cloisters incrusted with marble or radiant with fresco, its rustic palaces and gardens, whose persistent and solid verdure of cypress and evergreen oak seems itself like architectural vegetation. Against the pure blue sky and the green hills everything stands out in sharp contour, and as a painter would say "composes" admirably. In this happy variety of monuments of all ages and of all styles, there are two monuments which dominate and reign over the town and over the whole country —the dome of the cathedral and the graceful machicolated tower of the Old Palace; one the centre of the civil life of old Florence, and the other of its religious life. Around these two points are grouped the palaces of the signori, the houses of the citizens, the streets, the markets, the squares, the monasteries, the various edifices of private and public life—the whole with a fitness, a proportion, and an exquisite harmony, of which Athens possessed the secret, but of which not even a distant souvenir remains in the dull uniformity of nearly all our modern towns. There is something consoling and ennobling in the aspect of Florence, in this small fatherland of so many great men, who each developed his individuality and left behind him beneficent traces of his genius. Dante, Galileo, Giotto, Ghiberti, Donatello, Michael Angelo, Luca della Robbia—what names and what works gathered together in how small a space !

It is constantly of Athens that we are reminded in wandering about Florence, where our steps are ever returning to the Piazza del Duomo or to the Piazza della Signoria, which, by their striking originality, make us at once comprehend the double character, civil and religious, of this animated and curious history of Florence. The cathedral of Santa Maria del Fiore, Giotto's campanile, and the baptistery built on the site of a temple of Mars form a characteristic group of monuments raised by the state for the sanctification of all acts of Catholic life. Neither time, talent, nor expense has been spared to give these monuments great splendor. Vasari relates how for two centuries a succession of artists worked at the church of

Our Lady of the Flower, from Arnolfo di Lapo to
Brunelleschi, who crowned it with a dome, which
Michael Angelo obligingly declared "unsurpass-
able," but which is, nevertheless, far inferior to the
dome of St. Peter's. By the side of the cathedral
is the campanile which Giotto began with orders
" to surpass all that the Greeks and Romans had
ever achieved of the kind in the plenitude of
their power." Opposite is the baptistery, decorated with mosaics by Greek artists, and furnished
with most famous bronze gates "worthy to give
entrance to Paradise." All this is noble, fine,
magnificent, and simple, but utterly wanting in that
mysterious impressiveness which fills us when we
contemplate our Northern cathedrals. Whether in
church or castle, Italian Gothic bears no trace of
that rust of ages which seems to us inseparable
from a mediæval monument; it is a Gothic
which, in spite of its years, appears to be new;
a white-and-rose Gothic, more pretty than majestic. The cathedral of Florence is a vast mosaic
of precious marbles of all colors, relieved by sober
and exquisite ornaments, the whole very pagan,
almost entirely free from Christian inspiration,
and a testimony rather of the grandeur of the
Republic and of the magnificence of its citizens
than of their devotion.

The Piazza della Signoria is the most wonderful and the most unsymmetrical place in existence, and yet the effect of the whole is most

harmonious. Buildings and decorations, palace, portico, fountain, statues are grouped, one would say at haphazard, in one corner, and yet in this apparent disorder there must be a superior order, inasmuch as it charms us. The impenetrable mass of the Old Palace forms a contrast with the arched openings of the Loggia dei Lanzi, where the soft light of the Tuscan sky caresses the perfect forms of those most wonderful pieces of sculpture: "Perseus," by Benvenuto Cellini; the "Sabines," by John of Bologna; "Judith," by Donatello; "Ajax and Patrocles," and "Hercules and the Centaur Nessus"—a most pagan assembly indeed. But what a delightful idea, this *loggia*, this charming shelter against the inclemency of a climate without rigor, built for the signori of Florence for days of public joy, when they came in presence of the assembled people to promulgate decrees, to· distribute flags, to preside over national *fêtes*, and sometimes over national disgraces. It was from this *loggia* that the signal was given to set fire to the fagots that were to burn Savonarola; and in his cell, still preserved in the beautiful old monastery of San Marco, you see, beside the hair shirt and the prayer-book of the prophet, a quaint old picture depicting the aspect of the Piazza della Signoria on the day of his martyrdom, with the narrow perspective of the Uffizi Palace, the Hercules of Bandinelli, the Ammanati fountain, the equestrian statue of Cosimo I., and the Uguccioni Palace, which Raphael is said to have designed. All this stands just as it stood four hundred years ago ; the only change is in the aspect of the people, who now wear shabby clothes, ride in omnibuses, and pester the visitor with offers of photographic souvenirs. Florence is no longer the *irrequieta e romorosa Firenza* of the Guelphs and Ghibellines, of the Pazzi and the Medici. It is a quiet, moribund city, where industry has no great hold, and where the churches and the studios show that the flame is almost dead in the two great lamps of popular imagination, religion and art.

When the long, sunny June days arrive, the monotonous duties of daily life invariably seem to me so absurd and so unendurable that I determine, sooner or later, to revolt, and, a few hours after this determination has been taken, I find myself at a railway depot asking information about the next train for some general destination. This summer, I suddenly conceived a desire to see sundry German museums, and therefore started one night, in the Paris-Frankfort express, with my passport duly viséd. This latter precaution had been rendered necessary by the new regulations which had just been put into force by the German authorities, and which still oblige all foreigners who cross the frontiers of Alsace-Lorraine to be provided with passports, viséd by the German consul at a cost of 12½ francs each. During the first few months after the promulgation of this vexatious decree, the German consulate in Paris took in something like ten thousand dollars a month in fees for passport *visas*.

This fact I communicated to the purse-proud and polyglot German gentleman who was my neighbor in the sleeping-car, but, being also a patriot, he found this good round sum a source of joy. "It might," he thought, "ultimately help the new Kaiser to dimeenish the taxes."

My German neighbor was too patriotic, and as I did not see why foreigners should be called upon to pay the taxes of the Vaterland, we agreed to disagree and try to sleep. So the beds were made up, and we turned in. "Tackety-tackety, tack, tack, tackety!" went the wheels clattering along the rails; "Tack, tack, tackety, b-r-r-r!" Then comes a fearful jolt, and the car sways to and fro. If I could only get to sleep! What is the matter with this pillow? Is it too high or too low, too hard or too soft? The stupidest and most incongruous thoughts crowd into my head, driving away sleep. The wheels grind and grate, and then start again with their "tack, tack, tackety" sound that adapts itself equally to imaginary drum-taps or to the movement of the popular air from the last operetta. Patience! I shall get used to it in another half-hour.

Horror of horrors! My German neighbor is beginning to snore!—a fine contralto snore! Is it possible?—he is snoring a tune! "Die Wacht am Rhein!" This is, indeed, a patriot!

At four in the morning we reached the frontier of Alsace-Lorraine, and under the watchful eyes of long-legged, blonde soldiers and gorgeously arrayed officials, we passed, we and our baggage, into the Zoll-Revisions Room, where our passports were subjected to close scrutiny.

After this little incident our journey was resumed, and my German neighbor soon fell asleep, and snored " Die Wacht am Rhein " until we came within sight of the Niederwald Denkmal opposite Mayence, when he woke up with singular *à propos* and a new attack of "patriotismus," which lasted until we steamed into Frankfort station, where he saluted me quite "famillionairly," and jumped into a fine two-horse barouche adorned with his coat-of-arms, and with the person of a blonde maiden whom he pointed out to me as his daughter—a sweet creature of archaic outlines, like one of Lucas Cranach's models dressed in modern style by a pupil of Worth. Alas! why did I not flatter this patriotic German? Why did I not agree with him and develop his propositions for him with cumulative arguments? I might, perhaps, have sketched out a romance with the Worth-Cranach maiden, and so steered clear of *ennui* in sleepy Frankfort.

The first thing I did on arriving in Frankfort was to take my seat in the baronial dining-hall of the Hôtel X——, and to wrestle with the *table-d'hôte* dinner. Opposite me sat a very gentle and civilized German and his pale, blonde wife, whose delicate face was just beginning to yellow into wrinkles. This worthy pair, evidently well-to-do people, ordered *half a bottle* of Médoc, which they shared, diluted with much water, and seemed happy. Alas! this spectacle filled me with sadness, for it was a proof that the woes and mockeries of travel had begun. These good people would certainly have preferred their national beverage, beer; but the German hotel *tables d'hôte* are too stuck-up to permit beer-drinking, and the profits on wine are too great to be sacrificed. In some hotels there is a notice posted to the effect that if you do not drink wine the dinner will be reckoned one mark dearer.

After a tremendous one-o'clock meal, I sallied forth to explore the town, and found it gay, elegant, well-kept, and prosperous. The old town round the red sandstone cathedral abounds in quaint corners and picturesque narrow streets. The river, with its bridges, and its stream dotted with timber-rafts, the glimpses of the town and its towers and spires, the panorama from this point and from that—all amuse the eye and provide subjects for the photographer. On the quay called the Schöne Aussicht, or *belle vue*, I noticed on No. 17 a memorial-tablet announcing that in this house Arthur Schopenhauer used to live, and I have no doubt he had a good time there, his pessimistic point of view being just as conducive to happiness as any other. In the pursuit of happiness one of the chiefest conditions of success is not so much a point of view as a good stomach, and as Schopenhauer dined contentedly for many years at a *table d'hôte*, as his biographer tells us, I conclude that he must necessarily have been a man of singularly serene mind and imperturbable powers of digestion.

To judge from the display in the shop-windows, the Frankforters are especially proud of two things—the marble group of Ariadne in the Bethmann Museum, which you see reproduced in all materials from alabaster down to gingerbread, and the imperial family and the three emperors of 1888. I saw the three emperors—old William, Frederick, and young William—stamped on pocket-handkerchiefs, cast in bronze and terra-cotta, carved on the bowls of briar-root pipes, painted on porcelain pipes, embroidered on sofa-cushions, printed on fearful chromo-lithographs. Photographs of the Emperor Frederick on his death-bed, with the empress shedding big, pear-shaped tears on the counterpane, and, below, the inscription, " Lerne zu leiden ohne zu klagen," are sold by hundreds. As for the present emperor, his portrait and that of his wife and children are to be seen everywhere, the family groups being especially in favor. And what groups!—the ideal of a Putney green-grocer. The emperor, in uniform, with his arm round the empress's waist, standing on the brink of a photographer's imaginary lake, and the imperial children sitting in a " property" boat. A veritable sentimental German family group!

Towards nightfall the aspect of Frankfort be-

comes very interesting and amusing. The great
show street and promenade in Frankfort is the
Ziel, where the fine shops are situated, and where
the beaux and the belles walk up and down. At
evening, too, the cafés become evident, but they
are not audacious and flaunting like those of
Paris. As soon as the gas is lighted the curtains
are closely drawn, and some of the best cafés are
up one or two flights of steps, on the first or second floors: the Frankforter, like the Dutchman,
seems to prefer to drink his beer in private, far
from the eyes of the madding crowd, and the
spectacle of the street does not interest him.
Very wonderful are some of these cafés, notably
one in the Schiller Strasse: a monumental place
with wrought-iron vines trailing up cast-iron pillars and branching out ingeniously into incommo-
dious hat-pegs; a ceiling decorated with the signs
of the zodiac, intermingled with cupids, mon-
keys, and a vague " Temptation of St. Antony;"
walls adorned with frescoes in the style of Schnorr
von Carolsfeld; a stupendous bar presided over
by a statuesque lady of Flemish proportions; the
whole inundated with a blaze of electric light.
In this café I fought successfully against a gigantic glass of beer, and read the leader in the *An-
seiger*, in which the writer treated the subject of
" Boulangismus," and in a short column and a
quarter found means to quote Aristophanes,
Cicero, and Madame Roland, translating the orig-

inal in foot-notes for the benefit of the less erudite. Bravo, Herr Doctor! What a blessed thing it is to have frequented the University of Göttingen, and to have learned to be learned with ostentation!

With its irregular streets and irregular houses, some antique, with quaint gables and innumerable windows; some modern, surmounted by skeleton signs and meshes of telegraph-wires; with its multitude of Renaissance cupolas and bulbous spires, its green masses of shade-trees looming up out of the mysterious obscurity and contrasting with the glaring electric-lamp of some go-ahead " Restauration," Frankfort at night is suggestive at once of New York and of Nuremberg; it is a charming and not inharmonious mixture of past and present—of old-time ways and nineteenth-century progress.

But why come to Frankfort? To answer this question fully would require an historical dissertation on misunderstood genius. I have come to Frankfort to see half a dozen pictures in the Städel'sche Kunst-Institut; not the flat-tinted abominations of Overbeck, Schnorr, Cornelius, and the German school of the nineteenth century, which Baedeker considers to be so interesting, but the early German and Flemish masters, two Velasquezes, the portrait of Lucrezia Tornabuoni by Sandro Botticelli, a Madonna by Carpaccio, and an anonymous work of the Florentine school

of the fifteenth century. The sight of this last
picture alone has repaid me for my journey, and
impressed upon my mind a souvenir which I hope
will be as indelible as possible. On a very sombre green background is painted a half-length figure of a girl just budding into womanhood, but
still retaining something of that adolescent lean-
ness which Donatello and the great Florentines
loved to render. The body is loosely draped in
white, over which is thrown an olive-green man-
tle. On the brow is an azure band of trans-
parent gauze ; in the centre of the brow a jewel ;
while on the head is wound, turban-like, with
crinkled folds, a white scarf which falls over the
back of the neck and round over the shoulders ;
the turban is crowned with a wreath of box-tree
sprigs, and from beneath it the golden hair hangs
down over the shoulders in innumerable finely
waved wire curls, each distinct from the other,
resembling literally golden rain, through which
the light plays—a miracle of the coiffeur's art and
also of the painter's—not, it is true, of the painter's art as Rembrandt understood it, but as it was
practised by the primitive Florentines, who were
so keenly sensitive to elegance and minute splendor of raiment and ornament. This enigmatic
blonde maiden, with her dark eyes, her regular,
tranquil features, her dazzling shower of golden
ringlets so preciously displayed, her exquisitely
delicate hand, whose slender-pointed fingers hold

13

a bouquet of daisies and pansies—a dainty bouquet of five blossoms, and no more—is so fascinating, and, as the French would say, there is something so disturbing, so *troublant* in her slender
and almost meagre form, that when once you have
really seen and felt the charm of this picture you
have stored up a souvenir for life, to be guarded
jealously in the most select corner of your memory.

But I have, I perceive, wandered from the subject, and forgotten even to indicate the historical
dissertation which would explain my journey to
Frankfort. In two words here it is: If Europe
had not misunderstood Napoleon I. we should
have had most of the masterpieces of Western art
commodiously displayed in the Louvre museum
in the very centre of civilization, and so we should
not need to travel over the face of the earth in
order to visit unpronounceable "Städel'sche kunst-
instituts" in out-of-the-way towns in the land of
"patriotismus" and "leberwurst."

CASSEL.

Statistics show Cassel to be a town of some 60,000 inhabitants, and the indulgent observer would doubtless pronounce it to be an animated commercial centre. It boasts a vast railway station; a monumental " Regierung " or government palace ; a huge post-office ; and a handsome modern Bilder Gallerie, in the most approved Renaissance style, enriched with Greek ornaments, and surmounted by reproductions of the bronze winged "Victory" which is the jewel of the Museum Fredericanum. There is a steam-tramway at Cassel, and horse-cars, and well-paved streets. But all this is of little interest: the charm of Cassel is the old town, such as the electors made it ; the round Königs Platz ; the Gothic church; the Friedrichs Platz, with its fine eighteenth-century electoral palace, its statue of the Landgrave Frederick II., its Bellevue terrace overlooking the tree-tops of the Aue Park which Le Notre laid out—the Cassel that abounds in quaint old houses with pointed or convoluted gables, and in squares and irregular places planted with luxuriant shade-trees.

At the end of the Bellevue, which is naturally the fashionable promenade of Cassel, is a round temple, or belvedere, in the Neo-Greek style invented by the French architects of the eighteenth century. From here the view is wide-sweeping and imposing. Beyond the park you see the green valley of the Fulda fading away into the blue distance, where the purple hills close it around and form the horizon ; in the other direction you see the town climbing up one hill and down another, and finally sloping towards the old castle and the Fulda bridge, and joining the open fields. The comparison with Athens suggests itself : the Bellevue is the Acropolis of Cassel and the Bilder Gallerie its Parthenon. Doubtless this comparison must have occurred to the old landgraves who vied with each other in making these German Residenz towns centres of literary and artistic culture, and who ruined themselves and their subjects in imitating the costly splendor of Versailles and the magnificence of the Grand Monarque. In the making of Cassel there were three influences at work — feudal, French, and Neo-Greco-Roman—exemplified still by the old Schloss, by the Friedrichs Platz, and the Aue Park laid out by Le Notre, and by the triumphal arch of the Auethor and the new picture-gallery which is the outcome of the terrible Neo-Greco-Roman distemper which has been devastating Germany for now a century.

With all this, Cassel, the Cassel of the days of the electors, is complete in itself, with its castle, its archives, its library, its museums, its river, its park, and charming promenades. All that is wanting to make the town absolutely ideal is a handsome old landgrave at the head of a literary and artistic court—a landgrave who would ride in a gorgeous coach and have his servants dressed in gay livery. If while strolling one evening along the Bellevue the landgrave's coach should appear, and behind it that of the Chevalier Jacques De Casanova, recently arrived in the town with swindling intentions, nobody would be surprised or embarrassed. Like all the ex-Residenz towns, Cassel has retained something of its courtly past, and all the modern improvements seem to be mere temporary excrescences that have no *raison d'être*.

As you pass along the Friedrichs Platz of an evening you will see in the open loggia of a café a whole family—men, women, and children—sitting calmly around a few beer-pots, thinking matters over and looking for all the world like one of those family portraits by the old Dutch masters— a " Familienbild " by Gonzales Coques, for instance. Such a group might be taken as a symbol of the town of Cassel : it is an old-fashioned place, musing sleepily over the past and accepting the present without enthusiasm, as if it were all a dream.

Cassel an animated commercial town ! This is
not possible. One cannot reconcile these spacious
promenades and shady squares with serious business, except of such a kind as is indicated by a
frequent signboard on which is announcéd this
strange combination of commerce : " Wood, Coal,
Bottled Beer, and Potatoes " — " Holz, Kohlen,
Flaschenbier, Kartoffeln." And, after selling the
usual amount of coal, bottled beer, and potatoes,
the good tradesmen of Cassel light their penny
cigars, and, with their wives and children, take an
evening stroll along the Bellevue, admire the
" Schöne Aussicht," and so to bed. On Sundays,
too, in summer, they will take the tramway to
Wilhelmshöhe, to see the fountains play. And
so they pass their lives in sleepy, charming Cassel,
where even the spurs of the military men clink
discreetly.

Nevertheless, for the traveller of artistic tastes,
Cassel must always remain a place of pilgrimage.
The museum possesses a most important collection of pictures, including no less than twenty
Rembrandts of the first quality — notably the
painter's wife, Saskia Van Ulenbergh, dressed as
a bride ; the portrait of Nicolaus Bruyningh ; the
portrait of a man in armor ; and " Jacob Blessing
Ephraim and Manasseh." In order to see such
paintings as these one would willingly brave the
direst *ennui* and the most porcine developments
of German cookery.

NEXT after Nuremberg, Brunswick is noted as the finest mediæval town in Germany. This reputation is not undeserved; for, although it possesses few monuments worth speaking of, except the old Town Hall in the Altmarkt and some fountains of the usual slender, wire-drawn, old-German style, Brunswick is composed entirely of narrow, tortuous streets, lined with old houses with overhanging gables and irregular red-tiled roofs, such as you see in the background of Albert Dürer's pictures. And, curiously enough, these houses have been repaired and rebuilt for the most part in the old style, the only liberty taken being to put in some modern plate-glass shop-fronts. In this maze of narrow streets several lines of tramways run, with an occasional tinkling of bells as they round the corners; there are gas-lamps, too, and even electric lights and swaggering cavalry soldiers, and other modern improvements: still, the town retains its mediæval aspect. Every step we take brings us face to face with something picturesque.

So much for the old town, with its cathedral, its

castle, its Burg Platz, its Altmarkt ; but the ker-
nel of the town is all that remains, the shell has
been transformed entirely. The moat is navigable
for pleasure-boats and even little steamers ; the
ramparts have become fine promenades, laid out
as parks and gardens, in which has sprung up a
girdle of modern detached or semi-detached villa
residences, with bow-windows and conservatories,
where you see the worthy tenants sitting in solemn state, like manikins in a waxwork show,
watching the people pass and repass. On Sunday afternoon and evening all Brunswick is out
on the ramparts—on foot, in carriages, or on
bicycles and tricycles ; for cycling is in high favor in northern Germany, and I even saw some
young ladies with divided skirts riding tricycles,
and tearing along in the most ungraceful manner.

But in spite of this apparent animation, Brunswick is a terribly dull place for the visitor : in a
couple of hours you can walk all round the town
and through almost all the streets. Then what
remains to be done? Try the cafés? They are
about three in number, and all equally solemn.
Sample cigars? This would be too terrible an
operation, seeing that there are no less than fifty-
nine varieties of cigars at six a penny, all equally
deadly! Hunt the streets for a pretty face? This
would be chimerical, for everybody knows that,
except in Berlin, pretty German faces are rare.
Besides, one must be serious, and looking for

pretty faces in the flesh is not generally considered a serious occupation ; at any rate, one does not travel hundreds of miles to some out-of-the-way provincial town on such a frivolous errand. The great attraction at Brunswick is the museum and picture-gallery, which are now lodged in a magnificent new building — a model of commodious arrangement, like all the new German museums.

The antiquities and objects of art in the Brunswick Museum are not of the first importance, although some of the objects are of historical interest. On the other hand, there is a very admirable collection of Limoges enamels, and a very complete series of Italian painted pottery of the Urbino and Faenza marks. These objects, however, appeal mostly to specialists; while the average visitor will pay more attention to the picture-gallery, which is peculiarly rich in works of the secondary masters of the Dutch school. The pearl of the Brunswick Gallery is a life-size, half-length family group, by Rembrandt, which alone repays the journey. Against a background of dark-green foliage the father stands on the left; on the right the mother dances a baby girl on her knee, while in the foreground are two other children, one carrying a basket of flowers. The mother is dressed in deep red, and the baby-girl in rose-red. A rich golden light strikes across the faces, and touches the drapery in luminous masses. In this picture, so charming in its simplicity and *intimité*, Rembrandt has indulged in a veritable painter's feast of color. Technically, it is a most amusing and prodigious piece of work. But to give an idea of a picture in words is impossible. All I can say is, that I shall never regret my stay at Brunswick; the vision of this wonderful Rembrandt stored in my memory would console me for all the minor inconveniences I could endure in a twenty-four hours' stay in the town.

My first holiday ramble this year has been a run to Munich. The immense railway station is a model station, but vast, bare, and cold-looking. In a few minutes I am in the Maximilian Strasse, in an immense cosmopolitan hotel. The elevator lands me on the third floor; an elegant blond valet conducts me to a charming room, where my first movement is to look out of the windows. How amusing is this first look out of a high-porched hotel window, over the roofs and spires and towers of an unknown town ! On one of these roofs I notice two plumbers at work hammering zinc. They are whistling, the one treble the other bass, an old minuet. These excellent plumbers are evidently practised musicians, and their minuet is charming.

"*Table d'hôte* at 5.30," suggests the waiter. Unearthly hour ! It is now past 2 o'clock. There is time for a stroll through the town before dinner. Which way? I know not and it matters little. To know the way is to lose the pleasure of exploring. Maximilian Strasse? Very good ; I will go down this broad Maximilian Strasse, which seems to be the fashionable promenade and the fashionable shopping quarter. Here are picture-shops and milliners'-shops and tobacco-shops and cafés, colossal cafés with prim little waitresses dressed in black. Here the broad street spreads out into a square adorned with gardens and shady trees, and lined with tall, yellowish, stuccoed buildings in a sort of Tudor style of architecture. On the right, that immense building is the National Museum, the South Kensington of Munich. Then the street continues, between gardens and villas, until it crosses the bridge over the swift-rolling Isar, and divides into two branches to pass round the hill, on the top of which is built the Maximilianeum, a lofty pavilion flanked by towers and by a double tier of arcades and *loggias*. The summit of the building is crowned by a bronze Victory; above the lower arcades are busts of celebrated men, and the walls are decorated with frescoes now much deteriorated.

Following the shady promenade along the Isar, I arrived at the Zweibrücke Strasse, which runs almost parallel with the Maximilian Strasse and traverses the old town, passing under the Isar-Thor, which is one of the old mediæval gates and watch towers, very much restored and adorned with a long frieze in gaudy colors of no great artistic merit, representing a triumphal entry of Louis V. of Bavaria. Passing through this gate we come to the Marienplatz, on one side of which

is the new Gothic Town Hall, and on the other
sides quaint old houses very much bepainted and
illuminated with arabesques, just as you see in
the façades designed by Holbein. The column,
too, is a charming piece of seventeenth-century
work. It is of red marble, surmounted by a statue
of the Virgin, and at the four corners are winged
genii combating a viper, a basilisk, a lion, and
a dragon, which symbolize Plague, War, Famine,
and Heresy. This Marienplatz, with its column,
its Gothic Rath-haus, its steep roofs, pierced with
five or six tiers of attic windows, its painted and
ornate façades, and, at one end, the old Rath-haus,
the watch tower, and the antique gate barring the
way, has a strong stamp of ancient respectability;
indeed, it only lacks burgesses in mediæval costume, instead of in English cheviots, to present
the complete illusion of a street scene by Wohlgemuth or Van der Weyden.

My topographical instinct warning me to bear
to the right, I found myself within the precincts
of the old palace, with its picturesque courtyards
and fountains, frequented by gossiping maidens
whose babbling reminded one of the scene in
"Faust" where Lieschen at the well publishes her
"chronique scandaleuse" in presence of poor
Gretchen. Then, crossing the Maximilian Strasse,
I wandered through the courts of the old Residenz, which strongly suggest the quadrangles of
the Oxford colleges, especially of Merton; caught

a glimpse of the Hofgarten, surrounded by vast arcades decorated with mouldering frescoes, and so out into the broad Ludwig Strasse, at one end of which is a triumphal arch copied from that of Constantine at Rome, and surmounted by a bronze chariot drawn by four lions which obey the rein of a majestic figure of Bavaria. At the other end of the street is a reproduction of the Loggia dei Lanzi at Florence, and a church with a double campanile and humpbacked cupolas—a rococo church adorned with a profusion of dollish statues and complicated volutes, and reminding one of the Jesuit churches of Rome. The Ludwig Strasse, straight, long, broad, and magnificent, is lined on either side with yellow-colored stucco imitations of famous Florentine palaces. But enough for this afternoon; and, turning and passing with wondering eyes the Post-office, whose façade is decorated with Pompeian frescoes on a red ground, I found my way back to the hotel just in time for dinner.

I do not formally deny progress, but yet I venture to think that a *table d'hôte* dinner without a host is not one of the most brilliant inventions of modern times. I regret even the Old-World *table-d'hôte* Major, whose superficial elegance, threadbare anecdotes, and commonplace prattle, at any rate, gave a semblance of animation to the dining-room and helped to unfreeze the guests. It is bad enough to have to eat roast mutton with un-

dressed salad and green-gage jam ; but when you
are furthermore forced to eat it in silence, your
digestion is liable to be painful. This Munich
table d'hôte was one of the saddest I have seen.
The women chewed bread-crumbs to give themselves a countenance; the men looked gloomy and
scarcely dared to exchange a few words in a whis-
per, and an army of blond waiters, under the
command of a bloated chief, operated in military
fashion, each having his fixed post. At the sound
of an angry bell brusquely breaking the silence,
there was a tramp of creaking boots, and the various battalions marched out of the room. At a
second bell they marched in again, two by two,
one carrying a dish of meat or vegetables, the
other bearing aloft a bowl of sauce. And this
marching to and fro lasted for one hour and a
half.

Free at last, I escaped into the Maximilian
Strasse, sat down outside the hotel, and watched
the movement of the street, which was full of
promenaders, few of whom nature had blessed
with good looks. Soldiers abounded, of course,
and enlivened the gray street with their uniforms
of blue bound with scarlet and olive green bound
with carmine. What a profusion of salutations,
and, even on the part of civilians, what generous
and wide-sweeping cap courtesy ! I crossed the
road and entered a café full of military men and
civilians. Suddenly, having emptied his pot of

beer, a little fat soldier rose from his seat, buckled on his sword, marched to the other end of the room where an officer was sitting, danced round to full face, saluted, danced round again with a clanking of spurs, and then marched out with the air of a man satisfied with himself and conscious of accomplished duty.

What a beer-drinking place it is! One of the first things that struck me in my afternoon walk was the number of beer saloons and the multitude of servant maids whom I saw in the streets carrying glass pots with polished pewter lids and handles. These pots, I noticed, were invariably only half full of beer. Why so? Do the servant maids of Munich enjoy the right of drinking half the beer they buy, or are there no half measures? What is this mystery? Furthermore, I saw many soldiers walking along the streets carrying single pots of beer or series of twelve pots arranged in portable racks. In one of the passages of the old Residenz I even saw a sentry standing in his box and keeping guard over six empty beer pots. In the guard-rooms, through the open doors, I saw long tables dotted with beer pots, and soldiers hiding their faces in capacious pewters. In the cafés I saw civilians—men, women, and children —drinking beer, some out of glasses, some out of glass pots with pewter lids, and others out of gray stoneware mugs, also with lids. Why these distinctions? And each one, after taking a hearty draught, shut down the lid of his pot. In this café where I was sipping my *demi-tasse* these stupendous beer‐drinking operations were in full swing. What was to be done? How to pass the evening? I asked for a local newspaper to find the list of amusements; nothing but beer gardens! Beer, beer, beer, wherever you turn. "Hofbrau," "Englishes Café," "Spatenbrau," "Löwenbraukeller," "Grosse Concerte, brillante electrische Beleuchtung. Ausgezeichnetes Lagerbier." Evidently beer drinking was the chief industry of the Bavarian capital, and so it became my duty to visit the most distinguished soaking establishments.

The tramway landed me at Stiegelmaierplatz, and before me was an immense building resembling a mediæval castle nicely restored, surrounded by vast terraces and gardens, and adapted to modern requirements. This was the Löwenbraukeller; "accommodation for 6000 visitors; monster concerts daily by one or more orchestras; vorzüglich gewählte küche." At the little tables on the terraces were hundreds of beer drinkers in family and social parties. Inside the beer castle is an immense hall, whose open roof is supported by gray marble pillars festooned with gigantic garlands of greenery tied up with gaudy ribbons. The walls are frescoed with inscriptions such as this: "Trink Gesundheit Dir und Kraft—Beides liegt im Gerstensaft."

14

At one end of the room is a gallery for the orchestra; at the other a counter laden with beer pots, dough puddings, sauerkraut, steaming sausages, cold veal, green-gage jam, beef, ham, and all kinds of food; while the floor of the hall is occupied by row after row of brown wooden tables. Every seat is taken; some visitors are helping themselves at the counter; others are being served by ugly waitresses; the words "Ein moss! zwei moss!" re-echo from table to table; disks of brown felt are placed under the pots, and the adepts decorate the handles of their "moss" with a little plush doll or with a miniature escutcheon bearing the arms of their country—little knick-knacks which are sold by basket venders who walk about the room selling cigars and fancy goods. And whichever way you look you see people with paper napkins tucked around their necks, eating horribly indigestible food, drinking beer, talking, or listening to the orchestra which is playing the "Rheingold" and other gems of incomprehensible *ennui* from the repertory of the late lamented Wagner. Over the tables hovers a cloud of tobacco smoke, thick enough to dull even the glaring electric lights suspended from the ceiling. What a strange sight! What a picture of refined civilization is presented by this immense, dazzling, smoky saloon, with its swarm of men, women, and children eating and drinking; with its waitresses hurrying along carrying twelve mugs of beer at a time; with its newspaper sellers; with its frowsy old women who offer mean bouquets and buttonhole nosegays out of a soup plate! It is curious how little noise there is. There are no cries, no shouting of waiters, no clattering of dominoes as in a Parisian *café*. Even the applause is phlegmatic. As for the public, it is most decent and respectable and unsympathetic. The pasty-faced blond *habitués* who strut and swagger and wear strange hats are obviously conceited, but they are polite, but polite because they are conceited.

This is a typical beer saloon of the first order. In other less distinguished establishments you find a smaller orchestra or no orchestra at all. In some the waitresses are costumed; in some empty barrels do service as tables, but in all of them you see the same blond, bloated, heavy, bespectacled, calm crowd, smoking and soaking and pondering over the eternal antinomies. In a moment of hasty judgment one might be tempted to sum up and symbolize the whole sedentary life of Munich in a beer pot, and the active life of the city in a ceremonious salutation.

The next morning I started betimes further to explore the city. Crossing the Ludwig Strasse I followed the Brienner Strasse, which led me to a resuscitation of the Propylæa of Athens and two Greek temples in the Corinthian style, adapted for use as picture and sculpture galleries. Then, bearing to the right, I arrived at two immense

box-like structures, the new and the old Pinacothek. I spent the morning in the Glyptothek and
in the new Pinacothek. The afternoon was taken
up by another stroll through the town, visits to
the churches, and general inspection, and in the
evening I summed up my impressions.

Munich is a curious and unique city, for it was
not produced by the normal phenomena of the
slow agglomeration of human beings around a
central point, whether citadel, cathedral, market-
place, or port; nor has it grown up from century
to century, street by street and house by house.
Modern Munich sprang up, so to speak, in a night,
like a monstrous mushroom on a hot bed carefully
prepared and fertilized with the spawn of Attic
and Italian fibre. It is an entire city, planned,
begun, and completed by its founder, King Ludwig I., and enriched with churches, museums,
palaces, theatres, academies, porticoes, statues,
and ornamental architectural monuments of all
styles and of all ages. As you walk through the
broad streets laid out so admirably from the point
of view of advantageous perspective, the phantoms
of all the celebrated edifices of the world appear
before your eyes, one after the other, in chimerical
reality, unlike the models and yet similar; and
the more you look the more you are astonished
to find in one and the same town monuments
which you know are disseminated in so many different towns, and the sight of which has cost you

so many long journeys. For, like the Emperor Hadrian, King Ludwig I. caused to be built at Munich copies or specimens of all the famous monuments which had struck him in the course of his wanderings as an artist and a poet before he became a monarch. The idea was right royal and noble, and it must be confessed that the copies were executed with much taste, and, above all, with much erudition. And yet how much more delightful and interesting is the old town around the Marienplatz than the modern museum town where you see, here a fragment of Venice without the canals, and there a fragment of Florence without the pure sky, of Rome without its ruins, of Athens without its luminous aridity! St. Mark's, the Loggia dei Lanzi, St. Paul *extra muros*, the Propylæa, the Parthenon, have all been transplanted to Munich. The whole town seems to have been built as a homage to some mixed and pedantic Neo-Hellenic ideal. The very names of the buildings are Greek—the picture and sculpture galleries are styled Pinacothek and Glyptothek. And yet in spite of their merits the buildings of new Munich impress one as being utterly incongruous in such a climate as that of rainy Bavaria, and one feels no joy in contemplating here a Greek temple, there a Florentine arcade, leprous with mouldering and obliterated frescoes, and there a monstrous structure of yellow stucco in a pseudo-Tudor style.

The new Pinacothek contains a *résumé* of the curious artistic movement which produced new Munich. The building itself is absolutely hideous; it resembles in shape a gigantic Saratoga trunk, and it is decorated exteriorly with frescoes which wind and weather have happily effaced or nearly effaced. But the original oil sketches made for these frescoes are preserved in the gallery inside for the amusement and edification of posterity. There are eighteen of them, all comic in their sincerity, all celebrating the glory of the Mæcenas Ludwig I., and all illustrating the Helleno-Italic craze to which the immense error of new Munich is due. The funniest is an allegory showing Winkelmann, Thorwaldsen, and Jacob Carstens on one side, and Cornelius, Overbeck, and another painter on the other — the latter three mounted on a winged horse and charging, under the direction of Minerva, a three-headed and bewigged lion monster representing the "Zopf," or rococo style. These artists and learned men all have their hair smoothly combed and correctly parted, and over their 1830 frock-coats they wear blue, red, and yellow draperies nicely arranged in truly classical folds. Underneath the monster we see a tomb in which are imprisoned three classical maidens draped *à la* Burne Jones, who have been keeping alive the lamp of art in this narrow dungeon. As the "Zopf" monster has only three heads and one body, whereas the attacking artists have six heads and six bodies, to say nothing of Minerva and the winged horse, we feel sure on which side victory shall perch. In another of Kaulbach's sketches we see the "Studio of German Artists of the New School at Rome." Outside a ruined gate painters and sculptors with queer felt hats, long hair, and artistic cloaks draped over their old-fashioned broadcloth, are seen crowded together and standing in one another's light as they carve, sketch, and paint Transteverine models and Roman peasants disguised as Bacchuses or the goat-legged Silenuses. There they are, Kaulbach, Cornelius, Klenze, Peter von Hess, Overbeck, Thorwaldsen, Schwannthaler, Rottmann, Schrandolph, and the others who devoted their lives and talents to the most colossal and misguided effort ever made to resuscitate antiquity.

In the museums, in the churches, in the palaces you see the works of the famous Munich school of forty years ago, that school which enjoyed unparalleled facilities for developing and manifesting its talent, inasmuch as King Ludwig furnished not only unlimited money, but also unlimited wall space for decoration—acres of fresco and parasangs of canvas. And yet how pitiable is the result! Cornelius and his less illustrious contemporaries are all very learned, and fully justified their philosophical, scientific, and æsthetic pretensions. From a literary point of view we must say that they compose well. In the vast frescoes of the improvised churches of Munich the historian and the antiquary can detect no errors. Hesiod, Homer, the Bible, the Christian Fathers, Winkelmann, Ottfried Müller, Herder, Fichte, Hegel, Creuzer and his treatise on symbolism, are equally familiar to these erudite painters, for whom, as Théophile Gautier has well said, "art is little more than a kind of writing which they use to render their ideas — writing which is hieratic rather than demotic, and which one must know how to read. Orcagna, Gozzoli, Memmi, Perugino, Van Eyck, Dürer, Cranach, Holbein, are all well known to them; they do not disdain Michael Angelo and Raphael; the only thing they have neglected to do is to open their eyes to living nature, to look simply at men, women, and children, at the sky, at verdure, and at water."

It is indeed a curious fact that these famous Munich painters do not seem to have had the power of seeing anything directly. Their too perfect artistic education rendered them insensible to the actual spectacle of nature. They see everything through the eyes of their predecessors. Furthermore, few, if any of them, are painters. They seem to hate the palette, and when once they have expressed their idea coldly and abstractly in charcoal they leave their pupils to lay in the color. These men lack neither intelligence nor skill nor talent. But what they do lack essentially is the painter's temperament, which always betrays itself in the vaguest brush stroke; they have great powers of conception, but their sentiment of art is null. Take the greatest of the band, Cornelius, and examine his work; it is simply a vast mosaic of motives taken right and left; the omniscience of the painter has always a form ready made for his idea, borrowed from some masterpiece of the past; his work is like the city of modern Munich itself, a dolorous and incongruous patchwork.

One might examine the very interesting National Museum, the Bavarian South Kensington, and in the same way demonstrate that its influence has been perverted precisely by the spirit of erudition which Cornelius has bequeathed to his successors in industrial as well as in pictorial art. As an historical collection of national art the Munich National Museum is very remarkable, and its effect may be seen in all the shops of Munich: it has simply filled the industrial artists with erudition, paralyzed their inventive powers, if ever they had any, and reduced them all to slavery; for now their whole activity is absorbed in reproducing the ancient objects exhibited and ticketed and catalogued in their museum. The industrial art of modern Munich is, therefore, like the painting of Cornelius, and, like the city itself, patch-work.

But, happily, one does not go to Munich ex-

clusively to study the city and to see what to
avoid in art from the productions of Cornelius
down to those of Piloty and Gabriel Max.   The
great attraction of the place is its old Pinacothek,
with its rich store of works by the old Germans
—Wohlgemuth, Dürer, Schaffner, and Rogier Van
der Weyden : its gorgeous array of pictures by
Rubens, and its few choice gems by Rembrandt,
Raphael, Tiepolo, Ribera, and Pieter de Hoogh.
Munich is decidedly an interesting city—interesting because it is unlike any other city, and interesting also by reason of its irritating incongruity.

LIMOGES.

Limoges is one of those many interesting towns
of which the guide - books speak sparingly and
suggest that the tourist may see it thoroughly in
a single day. Doubtless. And the next day he
will have forgotten all about it. There are two
points of view from which Limoges is of very
great interest—first of all as a mediæval town,
and, secondly, as the centre of French porcelain manufacture. Modern improvements, broad
streets, and fine new buildings are not unknown
at Limoges, but the greater part of the town is
composed of narrow streets about two yards wide,
lined with quaint old houses built centuries ago,
with red and crinkled tile-roofs projecting over
the roadway, gables at all possible angles, timbers forming net-work over the walls, and Gothic
or Roman entrances with doors studded with
big nails like the doors of a prison. The general
aspect of the town is most picturesque. It is
built on two hills, that rise and form a sort of
amphitheatre, from which you see the river Vienne
winding through an immense valley. On the
summit of one of these hills is the cathedral ; and

on the summit of the other the churches of Saint Michel des Lions and Saint Pierre, each possessing fine and bold spires. The guide-books will tell you all about the churches and about the beautiful though sadly mutilated Jubé, in pure François I. style, in the nave of St. Etienne. These Gothic monuments merit careful examination; but, after all, one can understand that the traveller may grow tired of seeing Gothic architecture.

Let us, therefore, say no more about the churches, but rather ramble along the tortuous old streets and see the inhabitants and their ways of living. Starting from the Place St. Etienne, in front of the cathedral, we will bear to the left and descend the Rue des Petits Carmes towards the river. The more rapid the descent becomes, the more strange is the silhouette of the houses, with their red-tile roofs rising in tiers one above the other, with poles extending horizontally from the windows for hanging sun-screens upon, and with the upper story open to the air and forming a sort of *loggia*. The street is full of women and children, mixed up with brindled dogs and chickens. In the smoky interiors the fire slumbers on the hearth, but most of the domestic operations seem to take place in the gutter, for the street is so steep and narrow that vehicles can scarcely venture into it to disturb the inhabitants. Looking down the street, we see an old Roman bridge with half-oval refuges on each side, and beyond that the faubourg and green hills rising gently to the horizon. At certain hours of the day a procession of washerwomen, with clanking wooden shoes, labors up the street, bending beneath burdens of linen which they carry on their backs slung from a band called *serpelière*, which passes across their foreheads, their heads bound tightly with a kerchief of brilliant check cotton. The Limoges washerwomen occupy both banks of the Vienne, which are studded with slabs of granite, on which they beat their linen with *battoirs* in the shape of a flattened mallet. These hard-working women are the wives of the watermen who from time immemorial have lived in this particular quarter of the town, which is called Le Naveix, from the Latin *navigium*, according to local antiquaries. The men who live in this quarter are called *naveteaux*, and their business is to guide and collect the wood which is floated down the Vienne from the mountains up the river, of which immense piles are stored upon the banks. This custom of floating loose fire-wood is known only on the Vienne, and the curious weirs that we see just above the bridge are destined to catch it. One of these stockades, or *ramiers*, stretches across the whole breath of the river, and two smaller stockades are placed a few score yards lower down. The *ramier* is constructed of big tree-trunks planted in the bed of the river root upwards, and at an angle of forty-five degrees, the interstices being filled in with smaller poles. This hedge stops the floating wood, and the *naveteaux* in their punts drag it ashore with poles and hooks. This method may not be the best possible, but the oldest plans of the town show the *ramier*, and the *naveteaux* have always plied their curious trade as it is plied at the present day. This is a sufficient reason for leaving things as they are, especially in a town so respectful of tradition as Limoges is.

In all the other old quarters of the town the stranger notices the force of tradition. Limoges has remained in a great measure unchanged since the Middle Ages. The common people still talk the trilling and vibrating Provençal patois which we find written in the old documents of the thirteenth and fourteenth centuries. The favorite head-dress of the women is still the *barbichet*, which we see portrayed on the Limoges enamels of the time of the Renaissance—a white cap, slightly starched, with broad wings falling from the forehead and floating loosely over the shoulders. The very dogs of Limoges have a mediæval, wolfish look, with their rough, gray, brindled coats ; and the few horses that one sees in the old parts of the town are of the most unimproved and primitive lines. But horses at Limoges—and, indeed, in all the Limousin country— are not much used ; the beasts of draught are oxen and cows, which one sees, harnessed by twos and fours, dragging great loads by a simple band across the forehead, and without yoke or other harness. How obstinately opposed to progress these Limousins must be, one thinks as one sees their primitive teams. But the Limousin will reply that the ox is the traditional draught-beast of the country—stronger, more patient, and more economical than the horse. A yoke of oxen costs 600 francs, and after working three or four years the oxen may be fattened and sold to the butcher for 1200 francs the yoke. The cows, which may be used for light work, give every year a calf, which is sold for 100 francs; and after two or three years' work they, too, may be fattened and sold for meat. Furthermore, if any accident happen to an ox his carcase is always good for meat, whereas a horse that has to be killed is a dead loss. Finally, two oxen will pull a heavier load than four horses and pull it for a longer time. So say the Limousins; and their argument seems reasonable, and their business prospers; so let us say nothing more about progress, and admire, without criticising, the gentle yellow oxen that stride slowly along the Limoges streets with fern garlands hanging from their horns to protect them from the summer flies. Having observed none but yellow oxen in the country, I asked a native this morning if all the beasts were of this shade. "Mon Dieu! monsieur," he replied, "ce n'est pas defendu d'avoir des bestiaux d'une autre couleur!" But, he might have added, it is not the custom.

All the butchers of Limoges are members of five families; they all live in the same quarter of the town; and even now they form a corporation and observe certain usages and traditions just as their ancestors did hundreds of years ago. The archæologists see in these five families the descendants of the butchers who beheld the victorious legions of Cæsar, and whom the successive invaders of the Limousin country maintained and confirmed in their privileges on account of the usefulness of their services. Existing documents show that the butchers' corporation was legally constituted in the eleventh century, and since then their manner of life appears to have remained unchanged. Ask a Limogean to-day about the butchers, and he will tell you that, in spite of their sordid and filthy houses, and in spite of their poor appearance, the butchers are very rich, and that in the upper parts of their houses, where no stranger ever penetrates, "they walk on carpets" and live luxuriously. You will be told also that the butchers do not like to see strangers in their street or in their chapel; and, furthermore, that they are proud, quick to take offence, and not easy to deal with. These Limoges butchers have, in fact, been looked upon for centuries as pariahs. Until the last century no butcher married a woman not belonging to his caste; even to the present day, like the Jews in the past, they affect outward signs of poverty; and the idea that strangers are not welcome in the quarter of the butchers is a survival of the old usage and prejudice. Formerly, no one ever passed through the butchers' street; on the days and at the hours fixed by the consuls of the town, the butchers sold meat in the public market; then, when the market was over, they returned to their quarter, shut up their houses, and let their dogs loose.

The Rue de la Boucherie—or, as the natives call it, in reference to its shape, the Rue Torte—is, I suppose, the filthiest, the most repulsive, and the most picturesque street in modern Europe. It is a steep and very narrow alley, crooked, like a dog's hind leg, and lined on each side by queer houses, centuries old, with roofs projecting far over the roadway, walls built of beams and cross timbers, filled in with lath and plaster, and a third and top story entirely open to the air. The ground floor of each house is an open shop, the front of which is garlanded and festooned with quarters of animals, bunches of livers and hearts, bouquets of bladders, strings of red and bleeding meat, calves' heads, sheep's heads, tripe, and all kinds of carnivorous horrors. The counter stretches over the gutter, down which runs a foul stream, polluted with offal of all kinds, and under this counter the butchers' children delight to play, in company with the cats and the brindled,

15

gray, mediæval butchers' dogs. Above the counter
is stretched a ragged awning of bloodstained
cloths. The inside of the shops is as horrible as
the outside. Imagine a cave with blood-bespat-
tered walls, smoke-blackened rafters, and a floor
paved with irregular slabs of granite ! From the
ceiling the meat hangs from long iron rods, curiously twisted. To the left a narrow black staircase slants steeply into the upper darkness. At
the back of the cave a gate opens into a smaller
cave, perfectly dark, where, until lately, the beasts
were stalled and killed. Beside this gate is a
dresser with shelves laden with the family crockery; near by are the family chairs and table, and
at the big open fireplace the housewife does her
cooking. There are some fifty shops in this Rue
de la Boucherie, each one occupied by a member
of the corporation of butchers, and each one forming a queer picture, with strong effects of light
and shade, reminding one of Rembrandt. In the
course of all my wanderings, I have never seen
anything like this Rue de la Boucherie, or anything which gives one so completely an idea of a
mediæval street and of mediæval life.

The butchers are irascible-looking men, with
small heads, dull eyes, straight and delicate or
slightly aquiline noses, chestnut hair, long chins,
sensual mouths, and red faces. Their general
expression of countenance is rough and energetic;
their voices are brusque; but they are, neverthe-

less, kindly in speech and polite. The women are
small, pale, and anæmic-looking, and bear marks
of a race worn out by constant intermarriage.
The fact is that the butchers are all cousins. The
oldest family, according to the tradition, bears the
name of Cibot, and the others are named Pouret,
Parot, Malinvaud, Inge, and Plainemaison. Then,
in order to facilitate identification, each one has
a sobriquet, which becomes hereditary, like the
family name—thus, there is Cibot Parpaillaud
(butterfly), Cibot dit Boileux Père, Cibot Minet
dit gendre à Simon, Cibot dit le Petit Maître; the
Malinvauds are nicknamed Malinvaud-Chagrin,
Malinvaud-Pipe; the Parots are called Nâplat
(flat-nose), Chérant (selling dear), Fils du Canon-
ier; a Plainemaison bears the sobriquet of Louis
XVIII.; and a short Pouret is known as Tan-Piti
(so little). I need not add that these butchers
speak a Limousin patois which differs but slightly from the old Limousin dialect, and it is only
lately that they have consented to send their children to school and have them taught good French.

I have spoken of the butchers as still forming
a corporation, as they did in the Middle Ages.
And yet in 1791 all trade corporations were abol-
ished by law. How then has this of the butchers
survived? Through their obstinate fidelity to
tradition and through their religious propensities.
The Limoges butchers look upon Saint Aurélien
as their patron, and for centuries they have be-

longed to a Confrérie de Saint Aurélien, composed exclusively of the members of their families. In the middle of their street they have a chapel of their own, dating from the fourteenth century; they have their own *curé*, their relics, and their two great annual *fêtes* of St. Aurélien for the meat butchers, and of Notre Dame des Petits Ventres for the tripe butchers. At the time of the Revolution their chapel was sold at auction, together with the sacristy and dependencies, and bought by Barthelemy Cibot and Maurice Malinvaud. In 1827, when the country became once more settled, all the butchers, heads of families, numbering fifty-eight, declared, before a notary, that the chapel had been bought to be the common property of the butchers, and the price paid by all the butchers. It is this Confrérie de Saint Aurélien which keeps the butchers together. Every seven years they meet in the sacristy of their chapel, and elect a captain, a lieutenant, and two syndics, each of whom appoints four corporals. These officers form a sort of council, which watches over the religious, social, and commercial interests of the inhabitants of this curious quarter of Limoges.

The organization of this *confrérie*, as it was explained to me by the captain, is very complicated. It will suffice, to show how conservative and honest the butchers are, to say that the chapel, with all the working of the *confrérie*, is supported by fixed contributions and taxes levied on cattle and collected by the syndics. No instance is known of a butcher rebelling against these taxes or refusing to conform to the traditions of the *confrérie*. On the contrary, the butchers are proud of their traditions; and, in spite of progress, freethinking, anti-clericalism, and what not, they continue to regard the image and relics of Saint Aurélien as the Palladium of their homes and the guardian of their prosperity. They are even ready to defend Saint Aurélien with their knives and pikes; and the prefect and the radical mayor of Limoges have not dared to enforce certain recent anti-religious laws in the quarter of the butchers for fear of provoking desperate bloodshed.

The butchers elude in some way the French laws of succession. For instance, the eldest son always remains in, and keeps on the paternal establishment; but during the life of his father he receives no fixed salary. The father's authority is supreme, and he disposes of his property as he thinks proper. The eldest son never leaves the paternal house; when he reaches the age of twenty-three he marries, and his father keeps and lodges him and his wife, and allows him to sell certain offal, which brings him some six or eight francs a week. This is all the eldest son can earn until he succeeds his father. The other children leave the paternal house on the day of their marriage, and enter the service of other butchers, generally of their fathers-in-law.

In the organization, customs, and traditions of the Limoges butchers there is a curious sociological study to be made. I have only briefly indicated the outlines of their society, thinking that it may interest the reader and the traveller to know that there are still some remnants of the past that have resisted progress of all kinds, whether social, commercial, or hygienic.

WHAT a delightful sensation it is to escape from the closeness of a great city, to seat yourself commodiously in a railway carriage next the window, and to be carried with reasonable speed through a fertile expanse of hill and dale, dotted here and there with a clustering village and an old gray tower!   One is bent upon making a little tour—a very little tour, just a four-hours' ride—to see a Gothic cathedral.   As soon as you have passed the barrier of the fortifications, the country begins, and the green Marne River meanders over a broad valley, quitting and returning to the railway every few miles.   You see peasants working solitarily in the fields ; they rest on their spades and watch the train pass.   On either side, the track is lined with a brilliant hedge of flowers, poppies, lupins, sorrel, and feathery grass, running for miles and miles, and interrupted only by the railway stations.   As you approach Epernay, the country becomes more undulating, and the vineyards begin ; and soon you see in all directions nothing but hollows and slopes, sweeping away to the horizon, all bristling with millions of little stakes, around which the vines are growing. The aspect is not that of luxuriant vegetation, but rather of pale-green foliage seen through a veil of lilac-gray mist—an effect due to the gray, weather-stained stakes, the tops of which rise above the foliage of the vines and catch the light as the helmets of serried regiments drawn up in the sun. Sillery, Ai, Avenay, Rilly, are mere names of boundless vineyards, where vine-dressers, male and female, the latter sheltered by bonnets two feet six inches deep, tend with never-ceasing care the grapes destined to contribute so largely to the gayety of the world, literally and truly, from China to Peru.

As you approach Reims the vineyards cease, the culture becomes poor, and the town appears with a surrounding girdle of tall chimneys, in the midst of which the cathedral stands proudly out, topping them with its twin towers. At the station I was struck by the stillness of everything and everybody. The only sound was the gentle fizzing of the locomotive, the click of the greaseman's hammer on the wheels as he lounged along the train, and the twittering of the sparrows in the roof. The passengers, mostly business people, disperse calmly; in the station-yard a paternal gendarme converses in mute but expressive pantomime with a recalcitrant poodle, who has been infringing some rule or other; the omnibus-drivers and cabmen sit silent on their boxes and in no way

suggest that their services might be of use to you.
It appears that the Mayor of Reims, a great lover
of calm, has issued strict orders and decreed terrible penalties against obtrusiveness on the part
of the coachmen.   Hence this silence.

The town of Reims is clean, gray, and calm.
One cart passing along the great Place Drouet
d'Erlon re-echoes terribly, and the carter hangs
his head dolefully, ashamed at the noise his vehicle makes.   This Place, with its irregular houses
and pointed gables resting on wooden arcades, is
very picturesque, but it is the only part of the
town that has that quality in any noticeable de-
gree.   The rest of Reims is a conglomeration of
gray streets, looking very clean and comfortable ;
in the cottages in the outskirts you see hand-looms,
and men and women making merinos ; along the
Boulevard Ceres are fine houses with balconies,
where the rich merchants live, and beautiful public gardens adorned with rare plants and flowers
"placed under the safeguard of the public."   But
on the whole there is little to see at Reims except
the cathedral, the church of Saint Remy, and
the Champagne Cellars.

Thanks to the accidents of provincial hospitality, champagne was my first care and the cathedral the second.   On the outside of the town, in
the midst of gardens, are the champagne manufactories and cellars.   The one I visited was a
delightfully calm place composed of a garden of

ten acres, a villa occupied by offices, and an immense shed. Above ground there was little show; below ground there were some four million bottles of champagne stowed away in catacombs reputed to have been hewn out of the chalk bed by the Romans. In the 139 chambers of these lofty catacombs you see the various operations of the manufacturing of champagne, a natural process directed by the hand of man. The champagne manufacturers do not generally own vineyards; they buy the vintage from the cultivators. On the one hand, the French peasant loves the soil and refuses to sell his land; on the other hand, private and individual cultivation gives better results than cultivation on a large scale, where the care about details is less minute and less interested. In October the grapes are gathered, pressed gently, so as to obtain only the first and finest juice, and this juice is barrelled, and placed in the catacombs within twenty-four hours after the grapes have left the vine. This juice, like all the champagne wine grown on chalky ground, has two qualities, fineness and bouquet. In December, when this juice has become clear, the *assemblage* is made—that is to say, the juice of several different vineyards is mixed together, for each champagne vineyard has some particular qualities of bouquet, body, acidulation, or what not, by the proper combination of which the fine brands are obtained. This mixing is the most important part of champagne manufacture; on it depends the reputation of a brand; and if it is badly done, it may result in the loss of large sums of money. And so the head-cellarman, or *chef-caviste*, whose duty it is to taste and make the mixture, is a very important personage, although he goes about modestly and subterraneously, wearing an old cap and a long white apron. The *chef-caviste* is not often a man of literary culture, or even a practical chemist; he has simply acquired the art of producing and appreciating delicate distinctions of taste by experience and by the cultivation of a naturally delicate palate. The great champagne manufacturers acknowledge the services rendered by such a head-cellarman by paying him a salary of five thousand a year — 25,000 francs. The *assemblage* having been made, the wine is left in the barrels at least until the following May, and drawn off from time to time as the deposit sinks to the bottom of the cask. In May, we will say, the wine, being apparently quite clear, is drawn off into bottles, which are corked, and the cork clasped with an iron band. The newly bottled wine is left for a month or two above ground, in a moderate temperature, until fermentation begins, when the bottles are taken down into the catacombs and stacked horizontally, in cubic masses of ten, twenty, or forty thousand bottles, as the case may be. These bottles are left in the same position for two years, during which the wine continues clouding, fermenting, and depositing sediment. At the end of two years the process of shaking begins. Each bottle is vibrated every day, and at each vibration it is replaced in the rack more and more inclined with the neck downwards. The object of this vibration is to detach the sediment from the side of the bottle and cause it finally to be entirely deposited in the neck of the bottle on the cork. During this process of two years' fermentation many bottles are lost by bursting, however carefully the temperature of the cellars may be regulated, but the loss in these vast Roman catacombs is far smaller than in cellars of less extent and less profundity. The bottles, with their necks downwards, are now taken up-stairs and disgorged. In this process a man holds the bottle neck downwards and cuts the iron clasp. The cork then flies out, together with the foul sediment. The skill of the workman is shown in allowing all the sediment to escape, and stopping the hole at the right moment with his thumb. The disgorged bottle is passed on to the doser, who sits in front of an apparatus charged on one side with purified wine and on the other with sugar-candy dissolved in fine wine. After this dosing the bottles are corked, cleaned, and dressed for the market. Real champagne is therefore pure wine, made of the finest part of the juice of champagne grapes of different vineyards combined together and allowed to ferment naturally. The champagne *brut* is the pure wine corked directly after the disgorging operation. The dry champagne which the English prefer has about 1 per cent. of sugar candy added, and the percentage of sugar is increased to suit different tastes. The French require the addition of as much as 12 per cent. of sugar.

Such is a brief outline of the method of making champagne, as it is carried on in the obscurity of these catacombs whose chambers open one into the other through immense portals and passages that remind one of the rock temples of the East. Each workman, carrying his candle, moves noiselessly and works silently; the sound of a clinking bottle seems to sink into the dismal chalk walls without an echo; underground Reims is as calm, silent, and staid as the old town itself, whose Mayor prohibits the cracking of whips, and where recalcitrant poodles are brought up to comprehend the language of signs. It is strange that the generator of so much gayety should itself be generated so soberly.

The cathedral of Reims is the perfection and quintessence of all that is beautiful and imposing in Gothic architecture. The façade, with its receding portals, wrought, as it were, into a fretwork of figures; with its bas-reliefs, its pyramidal groups, its huge rose window, its majestic gallery of kings, and, above all this, its towers, is the most magnificent and splendid decorative ensemble of the kind that exists. The proportions, the solidity, and the lightness of this famous portal are wonderful. The hollows and reliefs, the ornaments, the open work, the windows and open lights of the towers without louvre-boards, through which you see the scudding clouds, the infinite richness of the details—all this is arranged so skilfully and so harmoniously that, while contemplating the huge mass with awe, one feels at the same time ravished with admiration and attracted more and more intimately the longer one contemplates it, so simple, *naïf*, and human is the whole of this splendid conception. And to think how far greater must have been its splendor when the sculptures of this façade were painted and gilded as they formerly were!—for we moderns only see Gothic architecture in its glorious decay, robbed of its color, except where that color has been perpetuated in the vitrified brilliancy of a rose or marigold window.

The façade of the cathedral of Reims has the advantage of being not only the most splendid conception of the thirteenth century, but also the only one in existence. That of Notre Dame at Paris is a façade of the transition epoch; that of Amiens is incomplete and built over at various epochs; Chartres is composed of fragments; Bourges and Rouen are mixtures of the styles of three or four centuries. The façade of Reims alone is pure thirteenth-century Gothic; its iconography is complete ; its innumerable statues have had the good-fortune to preserve their heads and noses in spite of years and revolutions. Its interest is inexhaustible : it dazzles you, charms you, astonishes you ; you leave it to examine the other parts of the building, and you return again and again to marvel at its beauty and to discover in it new beauties.

It has been the special privilege of Notre Dame of Reims to see all the kings of France travel down from Paris to be crowned there by the Metropolitan of France. It was through this portal that Jeanne d'Arc passed with her banner in her hand, which she had no need to dip, when she came to ask of the young king whom she had crowned leave to return and tend her flocks. Ah ! the *parvis* of Reims has seen noble company ! And on the façade, one might say that universal history, represented by its most renowned heroes, had taken up its post in every niche, and on every cornice and vantage-point, to see the crowd of the faithful enter the Church of Our Lady. In the centre, under a richly crocketed canopy, the Virgin is being crowned by her Son. The months, the great saints, the four rivers of Paradise, the elements, the ancestors of humanity, and multitudes of angels and seraphim, clad in tunics and copes and mantles, form the cortége of honor of the Queen of Heaven. Above the porches are colossal figures representing the Crucifixion and the whole history of the Saviour, the saints of the old law and of the new, the virtues and vices, the decent distractions appropriate to each season, the story of the Apocalypse, the story of Hell and of Paradise, the history of David and of Solomon, the baptism of Clovis, and the series of colossal kings.   In the decoration of the cathedral of Reims we may count two thousand three hundred and three sculptured figures of human beings and of animals.   What description can give an idea of the impression of such riches?   What words can convey an idea of the unity and completeness of the whole?

After the impression of grandeur and splendor, what strikes one most in this cathedral of Reims is the humor and human interest of the architectural ornament; it is the mixture of deformity and grotesqueness with extreme majesty and perfect human beauty; the ideally lovely figure of Eve—one of the finest works of French sculpture —and in contrast the colossal eagles with human legs that share the guard of the apsis with dogs, horses, unicorns, owls, and sirens.   Veritably all creation, both the creation of Nature and the creation of man's brain, has been called into the service of the architects of Notre Dame of Reims.

The interior of the cathedral is full of beauty and solemnity, with its vaulted roof, one hundred and twenty-four feet above the pavement, and its total length of four hundred and sixty-six feet.   In

the inside, as on the outside, the regularity and
unity are striking. The length is divided into
nave, transept, and apsis; the breadth into the
grand nave and two side isles, the height into
three stories, separated from each other by a
prominent moulding accentuated strongly even on
the slenderest columns. This determination of
the stories is a marked characteristic of the architecture of Champagne. It is to be found in all
the great churches of the country, built with rem-
iniscences of the Roman monuments so numerous
at Reims, in which the stories are always clearly
marked. But with all its beauty, the interior does
not fascinate us like the outside. After walking
around and around the basement, one climbs the
great towers and wanders in astonishment over the
roof to view with respectful familiarity the great
statues, fifteen and twenty feet high, that look so
small from below. One marvels at the immensity
of the building, at the excellence of the workman-
ship that resists centuries and centuries, at the
miracles of carpentry and of architectural statics
that were accomplished by the *maîtres ès œuvres*
who successively worked at Notre Dame. And
with admiration is mingled regret to think that we
have no longer the faith, the means, or the patience
to build Gothic cathedrals, and to think that Gothic
architecture is as much a relic of the past as the
Pyramids of Egypt or the Parthenon of Athens.
Here, at Reims, we see the Roman basilica, en-

16

larged, perfected, and having attained the maximum of architectural effect simultaneously with the apogee of the Gothic style. In this cathedral the system is complete, logical, and harmonious in its unity. The construction harmonizes with the decoration, the sculpture with the architecture, the painted glass with the dimensions of the windows : the form and the matter are inseparable. But the spirit of it has escaped us; its naïvely naturalist character is no longer either in our thoughts or in the skill of our handicraftsmen; its sculptural decoration cannot be imitated, and without its sculpture Gothic architecture is but a body without a soul.

On the way back from Reims the lover of Gothic architecture will not regret a visit to Notre Dame de l'Epine, a miniature cathedral situated half a dozen miles outside the old town of Châlons-sur-Marne, in the midst of a little village of 300 inhabitants. It is a delightful surprise to find such a beautiful monument in such wretched surroundings. The two open spires loaded with carvings, the innumerable pinnacles and crockets, the triple portal enriched with fine sculptures; the elegant interior, with its beautiful capitals, and, above all, its *jubé*, or rood-loft; the curious variety of the gargoyles—are all worthy of study, and the plan of the church as a whole is of extreme interest. The history of the church, too, is curious, and of all the more interest to us as the architect who built the

façade and the two towers was an Englishman
named Patrick, who agreed to accept six hundred
livres as his fee. The work was begun in 1419,
the stone was brought all the way from Lorraine,
and the church rose rapidly from the ground. In
1429 Jeanne d'Arc and Charles VII. drove the
English out of Champagne, and Patrick, the architect, took advantage of the troublous times to run
away and take with him all the money that had
been subscribed by the faithful for completing
the church. However, the zeal of the people of
Champagne and Lorraine was inexhaustible, and
so, in spite of the disloyal action of Patrick, the
church was finished in 1443. Such is the account
given by the present vicar of Notre Dame de
l'Epine. Will not some learned archæologist in-
quire into the matter and attempt to clear the
character of Patrick? The church which Patrick
designed and in part executed is so beautiful
that one is unwilling to believe the artist capable
of such an indelicate action as that of running
away with the cash-box.

At the end of the sixteenth century, King Henri IV. of France, accompanied by several persons, went to Aix in Savoy and bathed for one hour in the warm springs without taking any hurt, although neither his majesty nor his courtiers were accustomed to washing either in warm or in cold water. Still earlier, Julius Cæsar, whom the French familiarly call Jules, just as if he were a simple café-waiter, doubtless much troubled by rheumatism and lumbago due to exposure and camp-life, used to come to Aix for a cure almost every year during the period of his military exploits against the Gauls, Savoy being his road home to his Italian winter-quarters. The remains of the Roman baths still exist and serve a useful end, no longer as baths, but as the cellars where the Pension Chabert stores its wine, and they serve this purpose well enough, although the Barbarians knocked them about sadly at the time of their first invasion, thereby providing much food for conjecture and controversy to the archæologists of the nineteenth century.

Aix-les-Bains is a pleasure resort and a watering - place, and interesting from both points of view, but more especially important on account of the recognized efficacy of its waters in the cure or relief of rheumatic affections. The first suitable bathing establishment, since that of the Romans, was organized in 1776, but the great prosperity of the town dates only from five or six years ago, when the annual number of visitors reached the present average of twenty - four thousand, and the annual receipts of the Bath Establishment the present average of two hundred thousand francs. Savoy, it is needless to say, is a mountainous tract of country between Italy, France, and Switzerland; Aix-les-Bains is situated in the most beautiful of all the valleys of Savoy, at a short distance from the Lake of Bourget. It is a country of rocks, pine - trees, lakes and springs, both of ordinary water and of mineral water. Within a few miles of Aix are found the alkaline waters of Saint Simon; the sulphurous waters of Challes and Marlioz, and the various springs of Allevard, Brides, and Uriage. As for the waters of Aix, considering their natural temperature varying between 114° and 117° Fahrenheit, it is supposed that they must spring from a depth of about three thousand feet, and the level of the mouths of the springs is about eight hundred feet above the level of the sea. There are two springs, one of sulphur and one of so-called alum, the sulphurous principle in both being sulhydric-acid gas. The alum spring rises a little above the town in a vast grotto pendent with immense stalactites. Beyond the grotto is a reservoir, and a gallery, three hundred feet long, which conveys the water to the Bath Establishment. The sulphur spring rises in the Bath Establishment itself. The two springs together yield in the course of twenty-four hours some four million litres of hot water. In order to reduce the temperature natural cold water is added to the amount of three millions of litres, and so during the season the establishment uses seven millions of litres of water a day and treats some two thousand patients. The establishment, built on the slope of a hill, is a heavy and unlovely-looking place, having three flats with a façade on the primitive market-place, in the middle of which is an old Roman Arch and a fountain with three taps which pour forth night and day, for nothing, simple water, sulphur water, and alum water. This market-place, the steps of the establishment, and the entrance hall are a great centre of movement in Aix from half-past four in the morning until eleven o'clock A.M., when there may be seen a constant succession of men and women of all ages and all nations dressed in the strangest variety of undress costumes going to and fro, consulting the doctors, and vanishing into the cells that line the long, vaulted corridors of the Bath Establishment. The doctors of Aix have domi-

ciles and consulting hours, but until noon they
are never to be found at home ; you will see them
loafing in the vestibule of the Bath Establishment, waiting for their patients, catching them on
the wing, consoling them, listening to the same
old story for the thousandth time, walking a little
arm in arm, and otherwise kindly and affection-
ately entreating them. I never saw doctors paw
their patients over as the Aix doctors do. Such
appears to be the custom of the country.

Here come two rustic men wearing a semblance
of uniform and carrying a sort of Sedan chair, one
walking behind and one in front. The chair is of
primitive model and might be improved, but nobody seems to complain, and so it is likely to remain primitive. Over the chair is a sort of tent
of cotton stuff, striped red and white. The curtains are lightly drawn, and you see emerging
from the enveloping drapery nothing but a bundle
of blankets or perhaps a pair of shoes. Inside
the chair is a patient who is undergoing the water
and sweating cure. The porters have carried him
thus from his bedroom in the hotel or pension
where he is staying, and they are now taking him
to one of the cells or douches of the Bath Establishment, where he is placed immediately in the
hands of the tormentors. These douches are
well enough arranged, but, like everything else at
Aix, they might be better : they consist of a dress-
ing-room, from which you step down two steps

into the douche, where the tormentors, clad in
shirts, await the arrival of their victims amid a
mysterious arrangement of pipes and hydrants.
These pipes convey simple water and the hot
water of the sulphur and the alum springs.   The
victim sits on a low wooden chair with his feet
in hot water four or five inches deep on the floor,
while the tormentors, or *doucheurs*, propel heavy
jets of water all over the body at whatever temperature the doctor may indicate, meanwhile rubbing, kneading, and shampooing every part of the
body, thus stimulating the capillary and general
circulation.   The duration of this operation and
the strength of the water jets, like the temperature, can all be regulated according to the doctor's
orders.   The Aix *doucheurs* are famous for their
skill, and, in order to impress the simple-minded,
they say that their secrets have been handed
down to them from father to son and from mother
to daughter ever since the Crusades, at which period their ancestors learned the shampooing meth-
ods of the Orientals.   It is a fact that the occupation of the male and female *doucheurs*, or
shampooers, is hereditary, and monopolized by
certain families at Aix, but what secrets they can
have is hard to see ; they have doubtless a
special muscular development, great patience and
endurance, and singular delicacy and firmness of
touch.   Certainly in the treatment of Aix the
waters do much, but there is reason to believe

that the *massage*, or manipulation and kneading of the shampooers, does just as much if not more. As for the waters, in all probability the good they do is due to their warmth or thermality rather than to their mineralization. However, when the douche is over, and it usually lasts ten minutes or a quarter of an hour, the patient is rapidly dried, wrapped in flannel sheets and blankets, and carried back to his bedroom in the same primitive Sedan or invalid's chair. Having reached his apartment, he is lifted into bed, still swathed like a mummy, covered up with blankets and sheets, and left to perspire for a longer or shorter period. After twenty minutes or half an hour he may be rubbed down, dressed, and allowed to live like an ordinary mortal for the rest of the day. This post-balneal bed perspiration is not necessary in all cases, nor is the carrying in the Sedan chair obligatory.

Women are subjected to the same treatment as men, being attended to by female shampooers. Besides the douche, which is the most general form of the Aix treatment, there are swimming-baths of warm sulphur water where the patients are sent for a forty-minutes' soaking in water at a temperature of about 95°, with or without cold douches at intervals; there are also simple baths and all kinds of douche arrangements at different degrees of temperature and mineralization; two large inhaling-rooms, where the patients inhale sulphureous vapor in various ways; also spray rooms, where pulverized sulphureous water is brought to play upon any part of the body, especially useful in throat and nose diseases and wherever there is relaxation of the mucous membrane.

Now we come to Aix-les-Bains considered simply as a health resort and pleasure place. As regards scenery it is delightful; the lake of Bourget alone is full of charm, and there are dozens of most interesting excursions to be made in the neighboring country with Lamartine's " Raphael " as a guide-book. In this romance Lamartine makes Raphael select Aix as a residence because it combines the charm of the beautiful valley and fertile plain with the majesty of Alpine scenery. The district around Aix between Chambéry and Annecy, which is all within easy reach by rail or by road, does not exceed sixty miles, but these sixty miles are full of natural beauty and of objects of interest, and certainly the two lakes of Bourget and Annecy are not inferior in beauty to the famous Italian lakes of Como and Maggoire. Lamartine, with his charming poem of " The Lake," is identified with the lake of Bourget; at Chambéry one thinks of Jean Jacques Rousseau, whose enthusiastic description of the lake of Annecy has induced many to follow his example and build villas on its shores. Les Charmettes, half an hour's drive from Chambéry, will of course be

visited by all who remember the wonderful story
of Jean Jacques and Madame de Warens related
in his " Confessions."

As for the town of Aix, the best thing that
could be done with it would be to transport it
about a mile and a half down the valley, plant it
on the borders of the lovely lake of Bourget, and
connect it by a tramway with the Bath Establishment. This radical change will, of course, not be
made until some enterprising American comes
along, likes the place, and buys it. For the present we must be content with Aix as it is, a decent,
clean, and fairly civilized town, where you may
see at the same time in the semi-modern and
semi-rustic streets a peasant's wagon drawn by a
yoke of patient oxen and a duchess's victoria
drawn by a rattling team of Orloffs. In the
months of May and September Aix is an Anglo-
American colony; in the months of July and
August a meeting-place of French, Italian, and
cosmopolitan pleasure-seekers of all categories—
Russian princesses, numbers of Italian and French
aristocrats, diplomatists and statesmen, celebrated actresses, gouty journalists, and a swarm
of gamblers and *cocottes* who augment the apparent splendor of the daily spectacle and enable
the simple visitor to enjoy many luxuries which
such a modest town as Aix could never afford
were it not for that immoral but very productive
institution *la Cagnotte.* There are two rival casi-

nos here, each situated in a small park, each having a theatre, a restaurant, club-rooms, and gaming saloons. Each casino has an orchestra of sixty musicians, a theatrical or operatic company, and a numerous *personnel* of flunkeys in plush breeches and gorgeous livery. In short, both the casinos of Aix are very brilliant and commodious establishments, and during the season from May to October each one spends some $80,000 in keeping up appearances and amusing the public. The subscription to each casino is $8 for the whole season, but it is not the subscriptions that bring in the money, nor the restaurant, nor the café, but the baccarat-tables and the écarté-tables. In the course of an average year the *cagnotte*, or in other words the proceeds of the tax levied by the administration of the casino on every bank at baccarat and every game of écarté, brings in about $160,000 to each establishment. At Monte Carlo you see pious Britishers, who throw up their hands in holy horror at the mere thought of gaming, but who are still calmly enjoying the magnificent gardens and delightful music which a generous administration offers gratis to the public at the expense of the gamblers who are losing their money at the roulette-tables. So too at Aix-les-Bains, the splendor of the casinos, the music, the theatre, the flunkeys, and the beautiful gardens, are all paid for by those wicked men and gay women who crowd round the baccarat-tables, especially around the five tables of the Villa des Fleurs.

The reader will perhaps wonder how it is that public gaming is allowed in this way. The answer is this: baccarat and écarté are considered to be commercial games in contradistinction to games of pure chance in which the will or intelligence of the player cannot modify matters. Commercial games are allowed in clubs; part of each casino is considered to be a club, the entry to which is reserved; that is to say you have to go through the formality of asking for an admission card which is granted to men and women alike. At these baccarat-tables play begins of an afternoon about four o'clock, and may continue until two o'clock in the morning if there are players. At any rate, these two casinos in this peaceful valley of Aix remain open every morning until two o'clock, and around the green baize tables in the brilliantly decorated gaming-rooms you see a queer crowd of simpletons, adventurers, high-livers, honest women and dishonest women, all watching the game, and betting some one dollar and some a thousand dollars on the turn of a card, while the croupier repeats monotonously, "*Faites vos jeux! Les jeux sont faits! Rien ne va plus!*"

This mixture of fast life, of invalid life, and of the peaceful loafing and gazing existence of mere health-seeking idlers makes Aix-les-Bains a very amusing place wherein to spend three weeks.

Nature, the Alps, the pine-clad hills, green lakes,
blue sky, and moving clouds offer delightful
spectacles to the eye; but nature without man in
the picture is perhaps less conducive to health,
rest, and distraction than nature which serves as
a frame for an ever-changing picture of humanity
with the merest tang of polished and highly civilized rascality.

A VISIT TO THE GRANDE CHARTREUSE.

A THIRTY-MILE drive through some of the finest mountain scenery in Savoy and Dauphiné brings one from Aix-les-Bains to the gate of the monastery of the Grande Chartreuse, also known as the Chartreuse of Grenoble, which is perhaps more universally famous for the excellence of the liqueur which bears its name than for the exemplary piety of its monks. Before visiting the monastery I figured to myself the worthy recluses, in the intervals of prayer, all busy in the fabrication of their liqueur. I imagined some scattered over the mountain-side gathering herbs and simples, while others, in picturesque laboratories full of quaint alembics and queer retorts, were engaged in the processes of distilling, mixing, clarifying, bottling, and gumming on the well-known labels with the autograph of Dom Garnier. This vision was a delusion.

The Grande Chartreuse is built in a lofty mountain solitude, the approach to which is through the village of Saint Laurent-du-Pont, which is traversed by a rapid stream, the Guiers.

Following this water-course we come to Four-
voirie, a village at the foot of a huge mass of
mountains whose precipitous pine-clad flanks
are lost in the sky. Here the stream proves
to be a mountain torrent, but it has been dis-
ciplined to turn saw-mills and cement-mills. On
one side of the torrent is the manufactory where
the Chartreuse liqueur is made ; on the other is
a dismantled iron-foundery which the Carthusian
monks established in 1650 and carried on until a
year ago, their predecessors having been the first
metallurgists in Dauphiné, and Chartreuse iron
having been famous in the Lyons market as early
as the thirteenth century. Just beyond these
mills we enter the so-called Desert, or sacred precincts of the monastery, whose limits the monks
never pass when once they have taken their vows.
The road still follows the torrent, which sinks
deeper and deeper into a rocky gorge, while the
narrow path winds higher and higher along the
mountain-side, now under beetling gray rocks, now
through overhanging sombre pine forests enlivened only by a silvery cascade that gurgles forth
from the rock and leaps from ledge to ledge, as
it hastens to swell the roaring torrent dimly seen
far below through interstices in the thick foliage.
This grand, silent, and solemn scenery seems the
natural and appropriate road to the "terrible
solitude " where Saint Bruno went to establish
himself with his austere companions in the year

of grace 1084. For an hour and a half we mount
on foot, up and up, along this mountain road, now
crossing some aërial fairy bridge, now peering
through a tunnel bored through the mountain,
now creeping along the edge of a precipice, until
at last we issue from the dark pine woods and
damp rocks and enter a valley literally ablaze
with a thousand varieties of field flowers. Behind us, before us, all around, the mountains
tower up; we seem to be at the bottom of a vast
natural basin; and in this basin on the farther
slope we see the spires and steep roofs of the
monastery, an austere, unadorned, and solid mass
of white walls and black slate roofs, planted imposingly against a background of grisly rocks
and sombre pine woods. What solitude! What
isolation! What silence! And at once the
thought comes, what a terrible place in winter
time! We are here at an altitude of 3000 feet
above the level of the sea, and nine months out
of the twelve the snow caps all these surrounding
heights which shut the sun out of the basin during half the day in summer and all day in winter.
The name of Desert given to this solitude is significant indeed, in spite of the richness of the
vegetation, which has nevertheless a funereal hue,
suggestive of darkness and mourning, but it must
have been still more significant when Hugh,
bishop of Grenoble, first led Bruno to the spot
whose then obscure name Chartreuse was des-

17

tined to become famous all over Europe. The
mediæval writers have exhausted the resources of
language in describing the awful and terrible
nature and aspect of the spot, shut in among
naked and precipitous rocks, surrounded by sterile
mountains, and for a large portion of the year
buried in snow. Since then the administration
of woods and forests has helped to modify the
severity and sterility of these mountains by plantation, and now the aspect of the place is solemn,
romantic, and picturesque rather than terrible.

Why did Saint Bruno choose such a solitude, and
why was his order so successful that at one time
it possessed 172 monasteries, while even in these
degenerate days there remain fourteen Carthusian monasteries in France and nine elsewhere?
The date of the foundation, it will be noticed,
is 1084, just after men were beginning to recover
from the alarm caused by the belief that the
world would come to an end in the 1000th year
after the coming of Christ. Bruno was evidently
an enthusiast and a reformer. Warned by the
negligence and lukewarmness of many of the
older monks, he adopted for himself and his fol-
lowers greater precautions against the artifices of
the Evil One, namely, a coarse costume, the sub-
stitution of a hair shirt for linen, most abstemious
diet, and limitation of their worldly goods to a
just sufficiency. Nowadays the great source of
revenue of the Carthusian order is the manufact-

ure of the Chartreuse liqueur, which produces a profit of $100,000 a year. The monks might just as well make double the quantity of liqueur and double their profits, but they refuse to go beyond the limit of the needs of their order and of their charity, or to extend the field of their commerce in any way.

The entrance to the convent is of the simplest. Over the green-painted door is an image of the Virgin, and on each side images of Saint Bruno and Saint Hugh. To the right is a wing where the servants of the monastery are lodged, and to the left rooms for the reception of indigent travellers. We ring timidly, still deeply impressed by the tranquil and sombre solitude of this mountain refuge; the door is opened by a lay brother clad in white woollen robes; it is the janitor, the *cher frère portier* as he is called. Dear brother porter smiles upon us, invites us in, and commissions a rustic serving-man to conduct us across the courtyard to the Hôtellerie. The serving-man, clad in a blue blouse, heavy boots, a broad-brimmed hat, looking like a plough-boy, also smiles upon us and begins to talk with great volubility about that most useful and most common of introductory topics of conversation, the weather. The courtyard is neatly laid out in geometrical grass-plots and adorned with two plashing fountains, is closed in on one side by a vast edifice accompanied by four pavilions in the Louis XIII. style, with very

steep roofs destined to throw off the snow. The
monastery, it may be remarked, has been burned
down eight times since its foundation, and most
of the present buildings date only from 1688.
These pavilions served formerly as lodgings for
the priors who came once a year from the different provinces of the order to attend the General
Chapter. Entering a vaulted corridor and turning
to the left we were shown into a long refectory,
where another smiling lay brother, the *frère hospi-
talier*, received us, asked for our cards, and as-
signed us rooms, at the same time telling us that
dinner would be on the table at six o'clock. Our
rooms were in the section marked " Camerae Pro-
vinciarum Provinciae et Aquitaniae "—clean,
whitewashed, curtainless, and carpetless rooms,
furnished with a bed, a chair, a *prie-Dieu*, a
night-table, a table with a quart mug of water and
a soup-bowl for washing purposes, a match-box, a
crucifix, a lithograph of the Virgin, and no look-
ing-glass. For the use of this room we paid one
franc. The dinner was served in the " Aula pro-
vinciarum Franciae " and consisted of potato soup,
fried carp, an omelette, cheese, fruit, red wine in
abundance, and after dinner a glass of Chartreuse,
the whole neatly served, with table-cloth, napkins,
and other accessories of civilization, for the sum
of $2\frac{1}{2}$ francs. If one were " hard up " one might
think of boarding at this hospitable table for a
few months; there are, however, two objections:

the Carthusians allow no meat to be eaten in their monastery, and they give notice that they cannot lodge travellers for more than forty-eight hours, owing to the large numbers of people who demand hospitality, amounting, we were told, to some 7000 or 8000 every year. In the 18th century, it appears, before tourists had been invented, there were 6000 visitors a year at the Grande Chartreuse, and in the 12th century the documents of the house already speak of the great affluence of travellers, *frequentia hospitum.* The fact that things have been going on in the monastery just as they now go on during six, seven, or eight hundred years is one that constantly strikes the visitor to the Grande Chartreuse. For centuries and centuries travellers have received, according to the statutes of the house, a dinner of soup, two courses, cheese and fruit, "with which they must be content." After dinner they have saluted "dear brother porter," as we saluted him, and, begging him to open that they might go for a walk, they have inspected curiously the monastic buildings enclosed in their surrounding wall, running up the hill-side with here and there a watch-tower, reminding one of the days of ancient warfare and mediæval ballistics; they have contemplated the marvellous curve of the mountains that close in the amphitheatre facing the entrance; they have wondered at the pure light of the silvery moon enthroned in the cloudless, tranquil sky; they have watched the evening star sink below the jagged horizon line of the blue-black hills, and listened in the crepuscular stillness to the distant clanging of the cow-bells as the mountain cattle wandered home from their highland pastures bringing to the cloistered fathers their offering of foaming milk.

Quite as impressive and soul-stirring was the celebration of matins, at which we strangers were allowed to assist in a gallery in the chapel. We had gone to bed at nine o'clock when the gates of the monastery were closed for the night, and at eleven a good lay brother waked us up to go to chapel. Passing along a dimly lighted vaulted corridor, we heard a bell tolling, and mounting a few steps we found ourselves in a gallery at the end of the chapel. All was dark; the only lights were the candles burning in front of the altar and two suspended, feeble lamps. In the obscurity the form and plan of the church were barely distinguishable. Suddenly, as the bell tolled faster, there was heard the rustling of feet, and some fifty phantom forms, some in white robes, others wearing black mantles over their white robes, glided in, each carrying a little lantern, and took their seats in stalls along the sides of the chapel. Those clad in white were the fathers; the wearers of black cloaks were the novices. The bell ceased to toll; a few moments passed in silent prayer, and then the phantom forms began to chant psalms and liturgical exercises, prostrating themselves absolutely from time to time, so that they seemed to sink into the floor and vanish from sight. The Carthusians have preserved their liturgy unchanged since the eleventh century; they chant monotonously in simple notes of equal value, without fiorituri or ornaments—a chant so simple that it takes no time to learn to execute it. As the ancient statutes of the order say: " The occupation of the true monk being to weep rather than to sing, let us make use of our voice in such a manner that it will procure our souls that intimate joy which comes from tears, rather than those emotions which are the result of the chords of harmonious music." And so the Carthusians intone their liturgy most simply, in accordance with the severity and austerity of their order. And during matins the church is the greater part of the time in complete obscurity, for, except when they need the light to read, the monks pray and chant in the dark, and hide their lanterns in queer, tall sheaths, which also serve as reflectors to concentrate the light on the antiphonaries. No words can convey an idea of the impressiveness of this spectacle of the Carthusian monks in their white robes, kneeling in their stalls like the marble statues that pray on mediæval tombs. In the pious concert the visitor, perched in his dark gallery, distinguishes the strong, vibrating voice of the robust man who is yet mounting the hill of life, and the weak and faltering voice of him who is descending the hill towards death.   In winter, in summer, above the noise of the torrent, above the sound of the tempest, the prayers of the Carthusian rise heavenwards.   And as one recognizes in the holy words the explanation of all human woes ; as one hears these lonely monks, forgotten by the world and yet remembering the world in their prayers, one's thoughts return to the past, and to the great psalmist, who, in the middle of the night, at the hour when the wicked man is plotting crime, when the guilty feel remorse, when the poor and friendless suffer, lifted up his voice and prayed for the wicked, for the guilty, for the poor and for the friendless ; prayed for the dead and for those that are about to die ; prayed for the unhappy that they might hope, and for the happy lest they should forget.   And this prayer of the Carthusians has been offered up, night after night and century after century, for more than eight hundred years. In vain death strikes ; it cannot empty those stalls where the same pious spirits seem to be lodged forever in the same statuesque bodies.   Revolutions have come and overturned thrones and destroyed empires, but not one atom has been changed in the thoughts of these devout souls, not one word in their hymns, not one fold in their shroud-like robes.   And after us others will come and find what we found, and meditate upon this grand and pious spectacle, nor marvel that many a belated traveller, whom chance or curiosity has led to assist at this midnight adoration of the Eternal, has felt in his soul the desire to embrace the life of the Carthusians, and endeavor to vie with them in piety and abnegation.

We entered the church at eleven o'clock, and it was nearly two o'clock when the monks marched out with their lanterns, and we returned to bed to think over what we had seen. The next morning we were up betimes, and, guided by a lay brother, we visited the vast monastery and inspected its chapels, its library, its refectory, and, with much curiosity, one of the cells where the monks live. also the modest cemetery where they are buried. In one half of the cemetery repose the sixty-five Generals who have presided over the order, beginning with Saint Bruno, who died in 1101. These graves are marked by stone crosses. In the other half lie the simple monks, whose graves are marked by simple wooden crosses. It is curious to note the epitaphs of the deceased, who all seem to have lived to an advanced age, 80, 90, and even 100 years, which shows that an austere and abstemious life is not destructive of health. Architecturally the Grande Chartreuse is of small interest, and the reason is to be sought in the rule of the Carthusian Order. The idea of the Carthusian monk is to realize, as well as possible, on earth the kind of life which he hopes to lead

in heaven, and that life, he imagines, will consist
in three acts, seeing God, loving God, and prais-
ing God. This ideal he endeavors to attain on
earth by the study of mystic theology, by meditation, and by prayer and liturgical exercises. His
desire is to quit the world and to concentrate his
thoughts uninterruptedly on God. Hence the
Carthusian monasteries are generally established
in Deserts in the midst of mountains, far from
human habitations, and the internal arrangement
is such as to promote solitude. Contrary to the
general idea, while the Carthusian lay brothers
have worked in the fields and at various industries,
the cloistered fathers have always worked in solitude, in the old days at the noble task of copying
manuscript, and, since the invention of printing,
at intellectual or merely hygienic occupations,
though the Carthusians have never been very
famous for their erudition or for their writings.
As they work alone, so also the fathers eat alone
in their cells, except on Sundays and fête days,
when they eat in common in the refectory, but
without ever talking; during the meal one of
them chants a chapter from the Bible in Latin.
The Carthusian day is divided into three parts,
and the night into three watches, of which the
first and the last are devoted to rest, and the second to prayer and intonation of the psalms. This
second watch, or matins, is one of the severest
trials of the order, and a good brother told us

that it drove away many novices, who could not endure the physical strain of being torn from their first sleep every night in the year to go to the cold chapel and chant in the darkness two or three hours at a stretch. Old men may endure it, perhaps, but generally the Carthusians enter the order young, say at 20 or 25, and the trial is a hard one. Among the novices who are undergoing this trial at present, we were told by the good brother, are a young American, two Russians, an Englishman, and a German, for at the Grande Chartreuse all nations are accepted, if their faith is sufficiently strong and their piety ardent and sure. But to return to the Carthusian day: from 6 to 10 A.M. the monk's time is taken up with spiritual exercise and prayer; 10 to 2, prayer, meals, and manual work necessary for health (sawing wood or planing boards seem to be the favorite exercises); 3 to $4\frac{1}{2}$, vespers; $4\frac{1}{2}$ to $5\frac{1}{2}$, meals and prayer; then sleep, and five hours later sounds the first matins bell. Thus the Carthusian quits his cell only three times a day—for matins, for high mass in the morning, and for vespers in the afternoon. The rest of the time he is alone, and his occupations are pious exercises, and manual and intellectual work. Perpetual silence is not the rule of the Carthusians, and on certain occasions they talk together, and once a week they go and walk in the woods for three hours. In order to increase the

austerity of the Carthusian's life, there are fasts
and long periods of abstinence, and always complete abstinence from flesh and animal food of
all kinds. The Carthusians are the only Christian order of monks who practise this kind of
abstinence, which is the distinctive mark of the
community and the strictest of their laws. As
for the costume of the Carthusians, that, too, is a
relic of the past ; it is a long tunic of white woollen stuff, a scapulary of the same stuff cut up the
sides so as to leave the arms free, and attached
to the scapulary a pointed hood ; in other words,
it is a slight modification of the costume worn by
the Dauphiné mountaineers in the eleventh century, and I have seen even lately in the Savoy
mountains peasants clad with woollen stuff of the
same make.

The cells of the Grande Chartreuse are isolated
like those of the old Egyptian monks, and all of
the same model : they are sixty in number, and
they are built around the cloisters, and especially
along the grand cloister, which is six hundred and
fifty feet long, the vastest cloister in France, and
of very beautiful Gothic architecture. Over the
entrance to each cell is a letter of the alphabet
and a text of Scripture ; at the side of the door is
a little wicket through which the food is passed
in on a sliding tray ; and the cell itself is composed of two flats. On the ground flat is a vestibule, a wood room, and a work-room provided

with a carpenter's bench. On the other floor is a bedroom, oratory, and study, the whole very small, simple, and austere, and decorated with religious images and prints of the most inartistic description. It is a strange fact, which has been remarked, I believe, by John Ruskin, that no Christian whose heart is thoroughly set upon the world to come, and who is, so far as human judgment can pronounce, perfect and right before God, ever cared about art at all. Certainly the Carthusians do not love it, for nothing more outrageously inartistic could be imagined than the cheap lithographs and paltry religious emblems and prints which they have ever before their eyes in their cells. How different are these abominations from the lovely miniatures with which the old Carthusians used to adorn the manuscripts and antiphonaries which they copied before Gutenburg saw the light! Thus it will be seen, the austerity of the Carthusian order and the special features of their existence caused their monasteries to be built in a special manner and with a simplicity which excludes all ideas of art. The only exception is in Italy, where the Chartreuse of Pavia is a marvel of architecture and decoration. But one may say, generally, that the Carthusian monasteries never at any time exercised any influence upon architecture. At the time of the Revolution there was an interruption in the existence of the Grande Chartreuse. The monks

were dispersed; their library was ransacked for
the benefit of the library of Grenoble; and it was
not until 1816 that the monks were allowed to return to their monastery, which had become State
property. In 1880, when the Ferry laws were
passed, and the Jesuits and other religious con-
gregations expelled from France, the Carthusians
were respected, doubtless because they are a con-
templative, negative, and thoroughly non-militant
order; and so they still remain the tenants of the
State, with the right of pasturage and of timber-
cutting in the surrounding forests, the whole of
Saint Bruno's Desert having become State property since 1789. It is also said that the State did
not disturb the Carthusians because they pay annually into the treasury $500,000 by way of tax
on the alcohol they employ in manufacturing their
liqueur. The origin of this liqueur is wrapped in
mystery; the Carthusians do not seem to have
manufactured it until the present century, and
they profess to have secrets for its composition.
At present the liqueur is made by ordinary lay
workmen, who are directed by four lay brothers
delegated as superintendents, and charged with
the more delicate operations of mixing and tasting.
But in reality there is no secret. Duplais, in his
excellent treatise on the manufacture of liqueurs,
gives the ingredients and proportions required
for making yellow, green, and white Chartreuse,
the flavor of which is derived from melisse, a sort

of mint, mountain wormwood, tansy, angelica or longwort, balsam-poplar, mace, socrotine aloes, cardamom, tonkin beans, cinnamon, cloves, hyssop, peppermint, thyme, arnica flowers, coriander seeds, Alpine juniper, nutmeg, the whole macerated and distilled in various proportions, which are recorded in specialist treatises. But the chief point to be noticed about the liqueur, from the manufacture of which these good monks derive their revenues, is that it is a most diabolic drink and exceedingly alcoholic. With the aid of a man of science I have been able to analyze the three kinds, with the following results :

One litre of Green Chartreuse contains:

Alcohol at 85 degrees, ... 70 centilitres
Sugar, ... 125 grammes
Water, ... 22 centilitres

One litre of Yellow Chartreuse contains:

Alcohol at 85 degrees, ... 38 centilitres
Sugar, ... 250 grammes
Water, ... 46 centilitres

One litre of White Chartreuse contains:

Alcohol at 85 degrees, ... 52 centilitres
Sugar, ... 375 grammes
Water, . . · . . . . . . 23 centilitres

For the benefit of the innocent, it may be explained that alcohol at 85 degrees means alcohol measuring 85° on the alcoholometer of Gay-Lussac, which instrument is divided into 100 parts, o indicating pure water at 15° centigrade, and 100 indicating absolute alcohol. Thus 85 indicates alcohol containing 85 per cent. by weight of absolute alcohol and 15 per cent. by weight of pure water. Kirsch marks 50° on this instrument, and ordinary brandy 45° to 52°. These technical but easily intelligible figures will show the reader what a very strong and unholy liqueur Chartreuse is. And perhaps this fact of the great quantity of alcohol in the Chartreuse liqueur will explain the superiority of the products of the monastic establishment. The more alcohol there is in a liqueur the longer it requires to be kept before use. The Chartreuse of the monastery is kept in bottle three years before being sold, while the imitators, having smaller capital than the reverend fathers, and needing to turn their money over rapidly and often, sell a Chartreuse liqueur which is crude and unripe, though otherwise manufactured in the same manner as the genuine article. I have mentioned above $100,000 as the annual profit made by the fathers out of their liqueur manufactory, but I will not guarantee the exactitude of the figure, which seems to be far too small. Probably double that sum would be nearer to the truth. However, diabolical as the liqueur is, and decidedly not to be drunk by the mugful, the Carthusians make good use of the great revenues which they derive from its sale, and, although the pope exacts a large share of their profits, they always have abundant money left for charity.

PARIS in August has its charms, and yet, with the exception of a few fanatical *boulevardiers*, everybody who can hastens to abandon the city and to fly to the seaside or the mineral springs. The example is contagious, and, although one knows perfectly well that seaside *tables d'hôte* are a delusion and the boasted attractions of mountain-climbing often a snare, nevertheless one packs up like the rest. It is admitted that Paris is intolerable in August. So, happening one day to meet an old college friend on the Boulevard des Italiens, I proposed on the spot, remembering that he was once the pride of our college "eight," that we should try an excursion on French rivers. The proposal was accepted, and we started there and then to buy some maps and hire a boat.

The boat was not easily found. The French have not yet become a rowing nation, in spite of the persistency of Anglomania in France. The few decent boats that are to be found on the Seine and the Marne are the property of private individuals, mostly Anglo-Saxons, who have got them over from England. The craft which we

18

finally had placed at our disposal by the courtesy
of a friend was a half-outrigged, pair-oar, pine
boat, roomy enough to enable us to be at our
ease even with our hair parted on the side—a
boat that would stand a fair swell without ship-
ping water, and yet light enough for three men to
carry. The boat was sent by train up to Montereau, the point where the Yonne flows into the
Seine, our plan being to row some distance up
the Yonne and then to return down the Yonne
and the Seine to Rouen.

At Montereau, accordingly, we got into our
boat and started gayly up stream; but at the
first lock an inspector asked whether we had an
authorization. "What authorization?" "An authorization to circulate." We had no authorization; in fact, we knew nothing about authoriza-
tions; we were foreigners, ignorant of the customs
of the country. No matter; if we had no authorization we could not go up the river. Where
could we get the authorization? Well, travelling
as we were, we ought to have applied to the Min-
ister of Commerce for permission to circulate on
all the navigable water-ways of France, in which
case we should have been free to pass all the
locks in the country. The permission would cost
nothing; it was a mere formality. As it was, the
best and quickest solution of the matter was to
get a permission from the engineer of the first
section of the Yonne, at Sens.

This was irritating. Sens was thirty miles up the river. What was to be done? An idea struck me. In the lock with us was a train of empty barges drawn by a tow-boat. The inspector could prevent us circulating in the water, but he could not prevent us going up to Sens, provided we placed the bottom of one of the barges between our boat and the water. An appeal to the captain of the tug-boat was responded to immediately. The boat was lifted on to a barge, and we jumped on to the deck of the tug-boat, and went on. It was a bad beginning, and we felt not a little irritated at this inopportune reminder that we were in a country full of remnants of paternal government.

However, our voyage on the tug-boat was not so disagreeable, after all. But first of all let me explain the nature of the craft—the more so as I think boats of that description are entirely unknown in America. The boat is neither a steam-tug, nor a locomotive, nor a dredger, but a sort of combination of all three. It is an iron hulk pierced with port-holes and looking not unlike a gun-boat. In this hulk is placed a clumsy-looking steam-engine, and on the flush deck six broad-grooved pulleys, fixed, in sets of three, on two parallel axles. These pulleys are moved by big cog-wheels worked directly by the engine. Now, along the bed of the Yonne, between Montereau and La Roche, there lies an iron chain with links

about three and one half inches long. This chain
is caught up by a pulley at one end of the deck of
the tug, wound round each of the six pulleys in
the middle of the deck, and passed back into the
water over a pulley at the other end of the deck.
The tug is round at both ends, and moves up or
down stream, pulling on the chain and dragging
a string of ten or fifteen huge barges. The pace
is not very rapid, but the dragging power of the
tug is enormous. Of course the tug cannot quit
the chain; and when two trains of barges meet,
one going up stream and the other down, they
stop, the tugs exchange trains, and retrace their
course—the one that was coming up going back
with the down-train, and the one that was coming
down going up again with the up-train. The
chain from La Roche to Montereau is nearly
sixty miles long. The same system of towing is
used on the Seine, only with larger tow-boats,
between Montereau and Rouen, there being a
chain from Montereau to Paris, and another
from Paris to Rouen. The latter chain has an
unbroken length of about one hundred and fifty
miles.

We had a jolly time on board this tug, or *re-
morqueur*. The crew consisted of the engine-
driver and stoker, who remained invisible except
when we were in a lock, and three men on deck
—the captain, Narcisse by name, and Anatole
and Eugène, two handsome and muscular men,

one about twenty-two, the other about thirty,
who managed the steering.   At the first lock we
reached we all jumped ashore, and I "stood" drinks
in the lock-keeper's house—five glasses of strong
cognac, at two cents a glass.   All the lock-keep-
ers turn an honest penny by the illicit sale of
drink to the *mariniers*, or watermen.   No sooner
had we got under way again than Eugène brought
forth a wooden pitcher of red wine and poured
out glasses round.   Then Anatole insisted upon
our tasting his cooking.   It was his turn that day
to be cook.   The offer was so kindly made, and
the hospitality offered us on board was generally
so delicate, so polite, so sympathetic, that it was
impossible to refuse.   And here let me remark
the secret of the great social charm of the French
—their quick sympathy and great human feeling.
Here were these watermen, simple fellows, intelligent withal—still, mere watermen—bargees, as
they would be called in England: they knew
nothing about us ; we were perfect strangers ; yet
here they were conversing with us in the most
agreeable manner and treating us with as exquisite attention as the grandest seigneur could display towards his guests, and that, too, simply, naturally, without affectation, and out of pure good
human feeling.   Eugène's cooking was doubtless
good enough in its way, and, luckily, we had
country appetites ; nevertheless, a dish of calves'
lights stewed with red-wine sauce proved rather a

trial. We ate some out of politeness rather than out of relish.

With continual libations of pure red wine, incessant pipes, interesting scenery, equally interesting explanations by our three hosts, the hours did not drag. This is saying a good deal, when it is remembered that we got aboard the tug at ten in the morning and did not arrive at Sens until ten at night. But we had so much to talk about that the time passed swiftly. Anatole was a comic fellow. It was he who told yarns—very Rabelaisian yarns most of them, and he was peculiarly severe on the priests and on government officials. He told us about the mayor of Pont-sur-Yonne, who had a great idea of his authority. When the railway through the place was newly opened, this mayor, wishing to get on the train, put on his official tricolor scarf, went and stood on the track, and as the express rushed by he screamed out at the top of his voice to the driver, "Stop, in the name of the law!"

Captain Narcisse, on the other hand, was a grave person and a married man. His wife, he told us, must be pretty lonely, for, with the exception of two days a month, he had to be on board night and day. Still, *la bourgeoise*, as he called her, had her cow and her goat, and she managed to get on. He admitted that she must feel lonely at night. Captain Narcisse and the engine-driver were paid thirty-six dollars a month, the two other men thirty dollars, and the stoker twenty dollars. They all slept on the boat and did their own cooking. Captain Narcisse admitted that the pay was small; but he thought the life agreeable, and said that he and his comrades were very happy.

Arrived at Sens, we landed, and our *mariniers* conducted us to an inn at the end of the bridge over the river, drank three bottles of Burgundy to our health and our next merry meeting, and so we parted, they returning to the tug, and we sitting down to cold fowl and salad in the dining-room of the Tour d'Argent, kept by M. Barbara-Foucher. The next morning we were up early, called on the engineer of the Yonne, obtained without any trouble an authorization to "circulate," and, that being settled, we determined to spend the day at Sens, the ancient capital of the Senonian Gauls.

Sens is a picturesque and rambling old town, on the right bank of the Yonne, almost surrounded by undulating hills covered with vineyards, wood, and regular bands of varied culture, broken here and there by patches of dazzling white, marking the entrance of some chalk-quarry. The view of the town from any of the surrounding hills is magnificent. The white houses, with their red-tiled roofs, worn by time and weather to the softest tones, form an irregular oval intermingled with clumps of acacias and chestnuts and here and there a row of poplars. In the midst rises the cathedral of Saint Étienne, one of the oldest and finest of mediæval churches, while the Yonne winds along the edge of the town, its banks planted with immense trees, and spanned by a gray old bridge surmounted by an iron crucifix. The panorama is extensive; and no more charming background could be imagined than the cultivated hills, with their parallel strips of different shades of green, broken here and there by a long white road running almost in a straight line from the foot to the crest.

Sens was an important place before the Roman times. Quantities of Gallo-Roman antiquities have been discovered there which have afforded an endless subject of discussion for the local antiquaries. One thing is certain, that many of the houses in Sens of to-day have been built with stones that were used by the Romans in their buildings. Furthermore, as early as the fifth century of the Christian era, Sens became again famous for its monumental aspect, and in the Middle Ages the town was full of churches and convents, and was surrounded by fortifications, towers, and ditches, or *douves*. The ancient walls and gates of the city have been almost entirely demolished for the sake of the building materials, while most of the convents and some of the churches were destroyed during the Revolution. The consequence is that in modern Sens you can-

not take ten steps in any direction without remarking some relic of the past. Here is the Rue
Brennus; here is the Café Drapès and the Place
Drapès, named after an illustrious chief of the
Senonian Gauls; here is a Renaissance arch;
here a portal; here a mullioned window worked
into the construction of a comparatively modern
house; here is a butcher's shop and slaughter-
house established in the cloisters of an old convent. Turn into the court-yard of this old inn,
and you will find that the stable has a magnificent
groined roof, while the coach-house doors are
adorned with fine sixteenth-century carved wood.
All about the town are half-timber houses, and in
many of the streets may be found fragments of
late Renaissance wood-carving. But the most
curious house in the town is one at the corner of
the Rue Jean Cousin, which must date from the
end of the fifteenth century. The angle of the
house, forming the street-corner, is one enormous
piece of wood—a whole tree, in fact—covered
with the most curious and delicate carving. It
represents all the ancestors of the Virgin, from
Abraham downward. Along the other main
beams of the house are friezes of the most exquisite carving in low relief, foliage and flowers
intermingled with figures and grotesque animals.

The cathedral of Sens need not be described
here. In its *trésor* are many curiosities, some
magnificent tapestry, and some shabby old vest-

ments supposed to have been worn by St. Thomas à Becket what time he was taking refuge in the neighboring abbey of Sainte Colombe-lez-Sens. The archiepiscopal palace, too, must be visited, and the portal, with its exquisite tracery, must be admired long and closely. This portal is certainly one of the very finest specimens of Renaissance architecture in existence and alone worth a visit to Sens.

Unlike most French provincial towns, Sens has no bad smells. The limpid waters of the Vanne River run perpetually along the gutters of all the streets, and render the town one of the cleanest and coolest in France. The picturesque old streets, with their babbling *ruisseaux* and their beautifully clean paving-stones, are made still more charming by the aromatic perfumes that rise from the rich gardens between and behind the houses. Around the town, following the line of the old fortifications, is a shady mall planted with immense elm-trees. The streets wind and zigzag about in the most irregular fashion, and each shop has a sign swinging over the door or painted on the shutters. The people are clean and well-looking, but tremendous gossips and passionate anglers. Nevertheless, Sens is a busy and prosperous town, doing business in whiting, cutlery, tanning, wine, etc. But the French very wisely refuse to sacrifice everything to business; they will take their leisure and have their talk.

Our intention in starting up the Yonne was to go as far as Clamecy through the Burgundy wine and wood country, but, owing to the *chômage* of the navigation prescribed by the engineers for the sake of repairing the locks and weirs, we were obliged to abandon that idea and content ourselves with rowing down from Sens. Our first stage was to Montercau, some thirty miles, with seven locks and a longish spell of straight and monotonous canal. On the left bank runs a line of low chalk hills, and on the right bank are the vast and fertile plains of Lower Burgundy, which supply Paris with large quantities of grain. The villages are few and far between, and, with the exception of the picturesque Pont - sur - Yonne, they offer no particular interest. Still, thanks to splendid weather, we enjoyed our row immensely. The distance was accomplished in twelve hours, from 8.30 A.M. to 8.30 P.M., some six of which were spent in passing through the locks,—a most wearisome process.

Montereau, where we stayed a night, stands at the confluence of the Seine and the Yonne: its full name is Montereau-fault-Yonne—Montereau where the Yonne fails and is absorbed by the Seine. The town is uninteresting; the old thirteenth-century church is ugly and in a poor state of repair. The only fine thing at Montereau is the double bridge over the Yonne and the Seine, —a splendid old structure. This bridge was the

scene of the murder of Jean-sans-Peur, Duke of
Burgundy, in 1419, in the presence of the Dau-
phin, afterwards Charles VII., during a confer-
ence between them, and in spite of the precaution which had been taken of erecting double
barricades to divide the suites of the two princes.
Jean-sans-Peur's sword is hung up in the choir of
the church, and on the bridge is a black marble
tablet with this inscription :

> " En l'an mil quatre cens dix et neuf
> Sur ce pont agencé de neuf
> Fut meurtry Jehan de Burgogne."

Our next stage was to Champagne, through a
beautiful stretch of scenery—a short pull of ten
miles.   The weather was fine, but a violent wind
was blowing up stream and mounding the water
up into waves so heavy that we could not make
much progress, and all the time we shipped water
over the bows.   After three hours' work, we landed at the village of Champagne, and put up at
the only inn there, kept by " Malin, marchand de
vins.   Loge à pied et à cheval.   Restaurant.
Friture." So ran the sign. Half a dozen villagers
gathered in wonder on the bank to see us land.
I suppose such a craft as ours had never been
seen there before. We carried in our oars, sculls,
rudder, and two valises, not forgetting the demi-
john for our wine.   And then, having tied the
boat up, we undressed and jumped into the river.
The curiosity of the villagers reached a feverish

pitch. There were more than twenty of them on the bank now, watching us swimming. It is a curious fact that the people in France who live by the rivers never bathe, and very few of them know how to swim. The watermen, too, rarely swim. Our bathing, therefore, excited the greatest curiosity all down the Seine.

After the bath came dinner at the inn and a view of the country by the light of a brilliant sunset. Champagne is one of the loveliest spots we saw. At this point the Seine runs between sloping hills that come down almost to the water's edge. At the foot of the hills on one bank is Champagne, a picturesque village of five hundred inhabitants. At the foot of the hills on the opposite side is Thomery, with about twelve hundred inhabitants. The whole district is devoted to fruit-culture. Every house, every wall, has fruit-trees or vines trained on it. Pears, peaches, and grapes are trained along the public roads, while on the hillsides rows upon rows of white walls, with red-tile copings, are built so as to catch and husband every ray of sun. On these walls and between are trained vines and fruit-trees. The whole district is one vast garden. On the crest of the hills you see the immense trees of the forest of Fontainebleau, which covers the vast table-land over the heights. It is in this country exclusively that the famous table-grapes called " Chasselas de Fontainebleau " are grown. The value of the grapes sent from Thomery annually to Paris amounts to upward of two hundred thousand dollars.

The next morning, after a swim and a cup of coffee, we pulled back up stream to a small town called Saint Mammès, at the confluence of the Seine and the Loing. Saint Mammès is a great junction for canal and river navigation and an important barge-building place. In itself the town is utterly uninteresting. The Loing is only navigable for about a mile and a half, as far as Moret, but just below Moret it is joined by the Canal du Loing, which completes the communication between the Seine and the Loire, the Rhone, and the canals of the centre of France. Our boat being light, we were able to pull right up under the walls of Moret and to land in the cellars of the Hôtel de l'Écu de France. Farther progress up the river is arrested by tan-mills and flour-mills.

Moret is a delightful old place, and one of the very few towns existing where the mediæval for-tifications still remain in an intelligible state of preservation. The town consists of one longish street, with an antique gate and tower at each end, and on each side of this main street a maze of narrow lanes and passages, zigzagging in and out, with houses, stables, barns, etc., built at the most irregular angles. The houses are all white, with red-tile roofs and light-green shutters. Right

and left of the main street the modern town, with
its two thousand inhabitants, has outgrown the
old lines of walls, but at either end, and particularly at the end of the town skirted by the Loing
and its confluent the Orvanne, the old walls are
in a fine state of preservation. Of the castle
there still remains a huge *donjon*, or keep, which
has been carefully restored and converted into a
dwelling by some wealthy person of the neigh-
borbood. The view of the town from the bridge,
with the church, the *donjon*, the old gate, the battlemented walls, and the bastions, with the river
running at the foot, forms a delicious picture.

The church of Moret, very fine externally, was
consecrated, it appears, in 1166, by Thomas à
Becket, and, like the cathedral of Sens, it preserves
among its relics some of the vestments of the English saint. It is a beautiful specimen of pointed
Gothic architecture, but, unfortunately, it is almost
falling into ruins. In one of the windows there
is some splendid stained glass. The organ-loft is
a singularly delicate piece of Renaissance wood-
carving. The day we were at Moret happened to
be market-day. The market is held around the
church and in the street that runs in front of it.
As we stood within the edifice, admiring the
graceful slenderness of the columns, the elegance
of the vaulted roof, the apparent immensity of
the church itself, due to the beauty of its proportions, the sparrows and swallows were twittering

in and out through the broken windows, while
from outside penetrated the hum and buzz of the
market and the yelping cries of the peddlers rec-
ommending their gay ribbons to the country-girls.
The stillness of the church seemed all the greater
amid this distant and subdued murmur. Then
from time to time a sturdy tread would echo
along the quarried floor, as some rosy-cheeked
market-woman, basket on arm, walked up the aisle
to the chapel of the Sacred Heart or of St. Joseph, to say her prayers, bowing devoutly as she
passed the mural tablet so prettily and touching-
ly worded:

"À la mémoire des enfants du canton de Moret, morts
pour la défense du pays, 1870–71."

Then would come in one of the ladies of the
town and walk up to her *prie-dieu*, in the centre
aisle. The whole social history of Moret might
have been read in these *prie-dieus* by an experienced eye—some of them covered with plain
moleskin, others with velvet, others with bands
of wool-work, others with dimity, others with simple cane seats and unpadded chin-rests, some
carefully swathed in brown holland, others left
exposed to the dust, and on each one the name
of the owner—on this one written in ink, on this
one a card, on this one a silver plate: "Mme.
Fuzet *mère*," "Mme. Vve. Dubras," "Mr. Yon,"
"Mme. Dagron," "Mr. Ronfanneau," "Mme.

Gromer "— all the inhabitants, from the mayor and the notary down to the pork-butcher.

The market outside the church was a scene that would have delighted the painter Prout. The stalls are few. The butchers, hosiers, mercers, and some of the peddlers alone have primitive installations covered with scarlet awnings. Most of the market-people lay their wares out on the ground. Along each side of the street are laid planks supported on low trestles or on pails turned bottom upward, and on these planks are seated, in serried ranks, the country-women— one with a basket of eggs, one with cheeses, one with poultry, one with garden-produce or fruit. The costume of the peasant-woman here and in the north of France generally is simple and not unpicturesque : the head is tightly bound up in a multi-colored plaid kerchief, completely concealing the hair; the bodice is tight-fitting, with a *fichu* thrown over the shoulders, crossed on the breast, and attached at the back ; skirt plain and unplaited ; apron ; shoes, or *sabots*. Some of the old women carry umbrellas of the quaintest and most æsthetic blue and green shades. The women do not solicit custom, and seem more intent upon gossiping quietly with their neighbors than upon selling their butter and eggs. At noon the market is over, and you see the women trooping out through the old gate and over the bridge, most of them on foot, some in carts drawn by

19

mules or donkeys, others in primitive vehicles dragged by oxen.

Apart from the church, the gates, the walls, and the castle, there is nothing specially to be visited at Moret—the "antique and royal town of Moret-sur-Loing," as the natives style it—but the whole town is charming, and the memories of the place go back more than two thousand years. The Templars lived there; for centuries it was a favorite residence of the French kings; in the fourteenth century the English occupied the town; the famous Sully administered the finances of France from his retreat at Moret; in the convent of Moret a legitimate daughter of Louis XIV. lived and died—so goes the story; this unfortunate girl was born with such a dusky skin that her parents were ashamed of her, and shut her up in this convent, where she was known as "la Mauresse," as may be read in the memoirs of Sully and Voltaire. Finally, in 1815, Napoleon slept at Moret the night before he arrived in Paris to sit on a throne in the Tuileries. But, even were there no historical souvenirs, all this country from Sens to Fontainebleau is charming. It formed the old province of the Gâtinais—the Vastinium of the Romans. An old writer of the sixteenth century, Dom Morin, dwells upon the singular healthiness and populousness of the country and the longevity and intelligence of the natives, and proceeds to summarize the qualities of these parts in words which even now need no modification on account of the healthiness of the country. He says: "Our very glorious kings have not only been advised to choose this country for their sojourn and for the preservation of their health, but, furthermore, have decided almost from all time that their children should be born therein, the said kings having esteemed that it was greatly in the interest of the state to choose the air where should be born those who would have need of great prudence and prettiness of wit for the guiding of so great and flourishing a kingdom as that of France. . . . The good situation and temperament of the Gâtinais produces, above all the other parts of France, judicious men and well advised in all their affairs and courageous defenders of their rights. They have not bad accents, like the Normans and the Burgundians; they are modest and courageous, and, above all, the nobles and gentlemen are courteous, affable, and generous, being, for the most part, descendants of kings and great captains. As for religion, they are religiously devoted to the service of God, and few of them belong to the pretended reformed religion."

As regards religion, what Dom Morin said three centuries ago is true to a certain extent still. At any rate, we noticed a great difference between the people of the Upper Seine and the free-thinking, wily peasants of the Seine-et-Oise, the Eure,

and the Seine Inférieure. The people of the Upper Seine, too, are certainly more polished, and
their talk is clear and good, whereas when you
get near Normandy you find a terrible accent
which it requires practice to understand. As regards the populousness of the country, it must
certainly have diminished immensely both on the
Yonne and on the Upper Seine, and the proof is
that all along the banks of the two rivers you
constantly come to paltry villages of only a score
of houses, perhaps, but with a magnificent old
church. The fact is that the population of France,
like that of all the Latin countries, is not growing, while, on the other hand, the great towns,
particularly Paris, are constantly draining the
provinces.

After visiting Moret, we returned to Champagne, and slept there that night, our hostess
having previously begged us to sign the register.
This register was one of the fine old imperial articles which the traveller now rarely meets with,
even in the country, the police of the republic
being far from strict on the point of the inscription of travellers. By virtue of a law of 22d July,
1791, inn-keepers are bound to have this register
filled up as soon as a traveller arrives, even if he
sleep only one night in the house. The register
contains so many sheets of stamped paper, ruled
into compartments, in which the traveller has to
write his name, profession, habitual domicile, age,

date of arrival, place he last slept at, destination, date of departure, place of birth. Most of the visitors to Champagne appeared to have been ambulant singers, lyric artistes, Italian navvies, tinmen, and peddlers. Still, modest as the inn and its visitors were, we found clean bedrooms, clean linen, and abundant and well-cooked food.

Leaving Champagne, we rowed down through magnificent scenery, skirting the forest of Fontainebleau, as far as Melun, and then from Melun past St. Assise and St. Fargeau — the scene of Dumas's " Affaire Clémenceau "—Seine Port, the forest of Rougeau to Corbeil, and from Corbeil to Paris. This latter stage, with the exception of beautiful forest-scenery between Melun and Villeneuve-St. Georges, was without incident and needs no special description.

Our journey through Paris was exceedingly interesting, because it enabled us to consider the city in a new light—as a port, almost as a seaport. At Charenton the Seine is joined by the Marne and the canal of St. Maur, and the navigation begins to get busy, so that we had to be careful about our steering. Between Charenton and Bercy Bridge we see massed together vast timber-rafts that float down from Burgundy and the Yonne, with whole colonies of lumbermen on board, with their goods and chattels, wives and children. Below the bridge we admired the splendid new embankment of Bercy, and along

the water's edge, on the barges and rafts, we saw
hundreds of stevedores, the redskins of Paris, the
débardeurs, direct descendants of the old *badawrs*
of Lutetia, bronzed by the blazing sun. Down to
the Pont de l'Estacade the quays on each side of
the river, La Rapée and Bercy, are covered with
millions of barrels of wine and brandy in course
of being unloaded and stored in the immense
entrepôts that are kept cool by shady trees.
Nearly all the wine and brandy is brought to
Paris by water. Below the Pont de l'Estacade
we pass the huge lock-gates of the Canal St.
Martin, which passes under the Place de la Bastille and connects the Seine with the basin of La
Villette, the Canal de l'Ourcq, the Marne, and
the water-ways of the north of France and of
Holland. Past the Arsenal, the Hôtel Dieu, the
Conciergerie, the Pont Neuf, with its statue of
Henri IV., we arrive in the region of floating
swimming-baths and wash-houses, or *lavoirs*, with
their ceaseless noise of beaten linen and hum of
restless tongues. As for the baths, they are
simply human frog-ponds. Passing along the
Louvre, we arrive at the Pont des Arts, with its
crowd of idlers leaning over the parapet and
watching the washing of innumerable poodles,
and at the Port St. Nicolas, where a London
steamer is discharging a cargo of horns, which
will soon become unrecognizable in the disguise
of ingenious *articles de Paris*. Next we come to

the Quai d'Orsay, the great firewood and sand
wharf. Here is unloaded most of the wood that
is burned by the Parisians during the winter
months, and the sand and gravel used for the
streets and public gardens. Still pulling down,
we pass the commercial quays of Grenelle and
Passy, with their stores of coal and iron and
chemical products, and so to Auteuil, with its
ginguettes, concerts, eating-houses, and music-halls,
and, on the opposite bank, a big ship-building
yard, where the Seine passenger-steamers are
built. At Auteuil we left our boat and returned
to Paris to meet a third man, who was to accom-
pany us the rest of the journey.

Meanwhile, still with the idea of Paris as a
port in mind, we paid a visit on foot to the central "docks" of Paris. These extend from the
Bastille to St. Denis, along the banks of the Canal
St. Martin, the centre being the basin of La Villette. The sight is really interesting, and one
which, I think, visitors to Paris rarely see. The
docks of La Villette are simply thronged with
steamers and barges, and on either side rise tall
warehouses, immense grain-sheds, steam-cranes,
piles of barrels and cases, millstones, plaster of
Paris, etc. These two latter products find their
way even to America. The celebrated French
economist, Michel Chevalier, when visiting Buf-
falo, noticed a boat laden with millstones like
those quarried in the environs of Paris. The

captain told him that the stones actually came from Paris, and added that on the Erie line, in Indiana, Illinois, and even Michigan, French mill-stones from La Ferté-sous-Jouarre were used. As for plaster of Paris, the quarries of Belleville and the Buttes Chaumont owe their name of "Carrières d'Amérique" to the country where so much of their produce goes.

A glance at a canal map of France will show the immense importance of the port of Paris, and how Paris is accessible by water from all parts of France and Europe. By the Marne and the canal of the Marne you reach Strasbourg and the Rhine. The Oise and the three canals of St. Quentin, the Sambre, and the Ardennes put Paris in communication with the Scheldt and the Meuse, by means of which the coal-mines of Mons and Charleroi send their products. In another direction, as we have seen, the Loing and the Yonne open up to Paris, by means of their canals, the basins of the Loire and the Saône, and complete the water-way between Paris and the Mediterranean. The Yonne, which annually floats down to Paris six hundred thousand cords of wood, not only puts the capital in communication with Lyons, by the Canal de Bourgogne, but also with Germany and Switzerland, by the Canal de l'Est, which joins the Rhine between Basel and Hunningen. The river-traffic is simply enormous. The colonial produce landed at Havre finds its way up the

Seine to Rouen, Paris, and Lyons; the wool from
Australia and the ivory from Africa are landed at
La Villette before being transformed in the workshops of the Faubourg St. Denis; wine from Burgundy, Cette, and Bordeaux, sugar from the north,
oil from the south, farm-produce and grain from
the west, iron from the east, are all largely con-
veyed by water in craft of all kinds—in barges,
drawn by horses, donkeys, or mules, on the central canals and rivers, in *porteurs*, or steam-barges,
with paddle-wheels aft, or in trains of ten or fifteen barges drawn by steam-tugs or by the tugs,
already described, which drag on the chain. Between Havre and Lyons there are several rival
towing companies, but the most important is the
Compagnie Hâvre-Paris-Lyon, whose fine steam-
tugs and barges are always to be seen on the
route.

Having met our third man, and bought a capital map of the Seine from Paris to the sea, we
embarked at Auteuil for Rouen. Having now a
man to steer, we travelled more rapidly than we
had done while we were only two. Our first stage
was from Paris to Chatou, through Bas Meudon,
Sèvres, Boulogne, St. Cloud, Suresnes, Asnières,
St. Ouen, St. Denis, Epinay, and Argenteuil—in
short, through the environs of Paris, for here the
Seine twists and turns about so tortuously that
after rowing six hours you arrive about three
miles by land from your starting-point. The sce-

nery down to Suresnes is, however, lovely. From Suresnes to Argenteuil it is abominable, and at St. Denis the water is as black and filthy as that of a Black-Country canal. At Argenteuil the vines reappear, and the large basin of Argenteuil is the headquarters of the yachtsmen of the Seine. Chatou, where we spent the night, is a charming suburban resort, full of pretty villas and inhabited by wealthy Parisian stock-exchange people and tradesmen. At the Hôtel du Soleil d'Or, an old-fashioned, rambling inn, dinner, beds, and breakfast for three cost nine dollars—which we thought dear, particularly after our experience on the upper Seine, where even in the towns the charge for the same thing never exceeded two dollars.

The next morning we got under way at nine, dragged the boat over the lock at Bougival, and rowed, through splendid scenery, and with the terrace and forest of St. Germain on our left, down to Maisons-Laffitte, where we breakfasted at the Restaurant du Petit-Hâvre, by the side of a fine old mill. The walls of the inn, and of the kind of loggia where our table was laid, with vines trailing over the opening, were covered with paintings, as is the case with many inns in the environs of Paris, where often first-class artists have left some valuable souvenirs. Our breakfast consisted mainly of fried gudgeons. All down the river we ate excellent fish—eels,

perch, gudgeon, *brochet*, and various small fish
that made capital *matelotte* and *friture*. The
whole length of the river is divided into cantons,
and each year the right of fishing in each is let
out by the respective communes to the highest
bidder. This right of fishing means the right of
using nets, the right of line-fishing with a float
being unrestricted. The French are passionate
and patient anglers, and all the way from Paris to
Rouen there is a line of anglers on either bank,
posted, like sentinels, at regular distances. Another feature that struck the crew was the wonderful amount of washing done in the Seine.
Below Paris there are no *bateaux - lavoirs*, or
floating wash-houses, except in a few towns like
Mantes, Vernon, and Elbeuf; but wherever there
is a group of half a dozen cottages near the river,
there you will certainly find half a dozen women
kneeling in wooden boxes or fenders on the brink,
with a little stool or shelf in front of them on
which they soap and beat their linen with a *bat-
toir* before soaking it in the flowing stream. And
all the time the busy creatures gossip and gossip!

After breakfast and pipes at Maisons, we started again at 12.30, and, still skirting the beautiful
forest of St. Germain, rowed through a long stretch
of delicious scenery by La Frette, Herblay, and
Conflans Ste. Honorine, where we again met with
very rough water, which broke unpleasantly over
our bows. The whole country is like a garden:

the hills are covered with vines, and the villages built in terraces up the slopes, with generally a pretty old church perched on the top. At Conflans we landed, and accepted the hospitality of Dallemagne, Marchand de Vin, whose kitchen and cellar were excavated out of the hillside. Dallemagne offered us a round, flat loaf, called a *galette*, and some sourish red wine, called *gingly* —the wine of the country—which we found very conducive to quenching thirst. We drank it in a rustic room trained over with vines and overlooking the Seine. The berries were already swelling, and hung down in luscious clusters over our heads. From Conflans we rowed down to Poissy, bathed, washed the boat, and put up for the night at the sign of the " Esturgeon," where we dined admirably on a balcony overlooking the river. After dinner we went on to the bridge—an immense old structure of sixteen stone arches—and contemplated, by a brilliant moonlight, a river-and-woodland scene, the broadest and finest we had yet beheld. The day's stage was thirty-two kilomètres. Dinner, beds, and coffee in the morning, six dollars.

The next day we were off at 7.45, and floated with the stream between a series of beautiful wooded islands, whose banks were literally ablaze with bright-colored flowers. The hills along the river and in the distance presented an incredible variety of tints of green and a luxuriance of growth quite remarkable. Nothing could be more lovely than the river-banks, the sloping hills now variegated with vines and patches of miscellaneous spade-culture, the white rock here and there laid bare by the wear and tear of centuries, the scraggy poplars waving solitarily on the crest. We passed Triel, Meulan, and Verneuil—where "bow," strong in history, remarked that the battle of Herrings was fought—and stopped for breakfast at Juziers. Thence to Mantes-la-Jolie, where we landed to visit the fine old church, and thence through a stretch of poor scenery to Vétheuil, where we put up for the night at a mediocre inn, "Nouveau Cheval Blanc," up in the village away from the river. However, we had a good dinner and were well treated. Our arrival in this village excited intense curiosity, and, while we were eating, a row of natives drew up in front of the door to catch a glimpse of *les Anglais*. Our stage this day was fifty kilomètres.

We left Vétheuil at 7.45 A.M. The country continued to be fertile, with hills on one side of the river and plains on the other. At La Roche-Guyon we admired the ruins of an old feudal castle. Thence through charming scenery to Vernon, where we breakfasted at an inn on the river-side. Our hostess was a fat, motherly person in a white cap, named "la mère" Rozé, who served us a splendid breakfast, sat down to table with us to watch us eat, called us her little children—

"*Mangez bien, mes petits enfants ! . . . Eh bien ! C'est-y bonne, l'omelette, mes enfants ?*"—was desirous of obtaining information about the Queen of England and the Scotch national dress, had views of her own about the Egyptian question, and altogether was quite a type.

After breakfast we rowed and sculled to Petit Andelys through delicious woodland scenery. Just before you reach Petit Andelys you pass King Richard's famous Château-Gaillard, a fine old ruin standing imposingly on the hill-top and commanding an immense panorama of hill and valley. At Petit Andelys we put up at the Chaîne d'Or, a fine and quaint old inn, with a charming old hostess who fed and lodged us splendidly. Our stage this day was forty-six kilomètres.

The next morning we were off at 7.50, and rowed for several hours through perfectly idyllic scenery, hearing nothing but the plashing of our oars, the cooing of the ring-doves, the whirring of the wings of a startled water-hen, and the whispering of the poplars. Arrived at the village of Tournedos, we landed, and breakfasted at an inn which was at the same time the grocery-store, tobacco-shop, and newspaper-shop of the village. Our hostess was an old Norman peasant, burned by the sun to the color of chocolate. With her head bound up in a kerchief, she looked not unlike an Egyptian mummy. She gave us an immense breakfast, in the consumption of which we spent nearly three hours. We did not get on board again until three o'clock. At the lock of Poses we were nearly crushed to jelly through a barge swinging loose while the water was sinking. Then we had a hardish pull to Elbeuf, where we arrived at 8.15 P.M., having been greatly delayed and irritated by the locks. We stayed at the Hôtel de France, and were well treated. The town is old, but far from prosperous. Our stage this day was forty-six kilomètres.

At Elbeuf our journey was practically at an end, the distance from there to Rouen being only twenty-two kilomètres, through comparatively poor scenery. Arrived at Rouen, we put the boat on board a steamer and sent it back to Paris, while we put up at a fine hotel on the quay, where we spent a few days in high luxury. Of the sights of Rouen I need say nothing. Are they not described in innumerable guide-books?

The whole distance we rowed, from Sens to Rouen, was about four hundred kilomètres, or two hundred and fifty miles. The number of locks, if I remember rightly, is twenty-five. These locks are the great nuisance of the journey. They are so immense that it takes at least an hour and a half to get through some of them; and the approaches to many are so awkward that, unless one's boat be very light indeed, one scarcely has the alternative of carrying it over the weir. I may say that pleasure navigation is hardly recognized on the Seine, and pleasure-boats have no privileges as they do on the Thames. They have to take their chance; and a poor chance it is when they have to pass a lock with ten or fifteen huge barges in it.

However, all these little dangers and inconveniences do not last long, and are soon forgotten. The trip is certainly worth making, and with a light boat it would be simply ideal. What more can be desired than exquisite scenery, kind and obliging people, abundant food, clean linen, and fine weather? All this we had, and more besides —that charm of novelty and of the unforeseen peculiar to "foraine travell."

FINIS.

www.ingramcontent.com/pod-product-compliance
Lightning Source LLC
Chambersburg PA
CBHW031043120726
47905CB00007B/2290